Gooseberry

Vickie

Patch Co.

A Country Store In Your Mailbox℠

Coming Home for Christmas

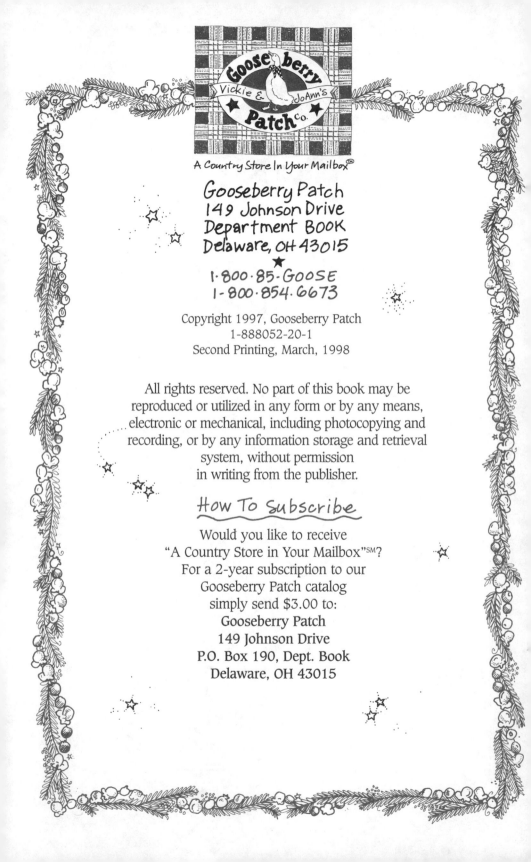

A Country Store In Your Mailbox℠

Gooseberry Patch
149 Johnson Drive
Department BOOK
Delaware, OH 43015
★
1·800·85·GOOSE
1-800·854·6673

Copyright 1997, Gooseberry Patch
1-888052-20-1
Second Printing, March, 1998

How To Subscribe

Would you like to receive
"A Country Store in Your Mailbox"℠?
For a 2-year subscription to our
Gooseberry Patch catalog
simply send $3.00 to:
Gooseberry Patch
149 Johnson Drive
P.O. Box 190, Dept. Book
Delaware, OH 43015

Contents

Memories of Christmas Past 5

A Sprinkle Here, A Sparkle There
    Easy Home Decorating Ideas 24
    Magical Holiday Crafts 36

Make It Merry, Wrap It Bright
    Gifts From Your Christmas Kitchen 52

A Feast of Time-tested Recipes
    Christmas Morn Delights 74
    Appetizers & Yuletide Beverages 94
    Hearty Soups & Bountiful Breads 114
    Memorable Main Dishes 132
    Delectable Desserts 172
    Cookies, Cookies, Cookies 192

Dedication

To the child that lives in all of us,
on Christmas morn and always.

Appreciation

To our generous country friends
who shared their golden memories, personal joys,
clever ideas and Grandmothers' recipes,
we thank you!

Memories of Christmas Past

Memories

Melanie Elmore
Schenectady, NY

Christmas Memories in my Heart

Baking cookies, Mom and me, wearing aprons, sipping tea
Sugar sprinkles, cinnamon smells, a favorite recipe, little bells
Sharing nibbles, frosted trees, stars in a row for Dad to see.

I wrote this poem in memory of my mom, who passed away three years ago. The time Mom and I spent baking cookies together will always be my favorite Christmas memory. I have a special affection for the sugar cookies we baked, probably because they were the first cookie I learned to make and the most fun to decorate. We used the same recipe year after year, and now I am the proud owner of her well-worn cookbook. The recipe is circled with a note from Mom in the margin that reads, "This one Melanie," just in case I forget which one to use.

Mom and I started a tradition of spending one day together, usually the week before Christmas, to bake batches of cookies. Our day started by reading through volumes of cookie books and magazines to find new and exciting cookies to make. Then we'd don our special holiday aprons, drink lots of tea, listen to Christmas music and bake away! When the last batch was out of the oven and the last cookie frosted, Dad was invited into the kitchen to sample and "ooh and ahh" over the day's accomplishments.

I keep these wonderful memories alive by decorating a small tree I keep on a pie pantry in my kitchen. On it I've hung my favorite cookie cutters from my mom's collection, along with this poem, glued inside a red heart cookie cutter.

My memory tree is both a reminder of my wonderful Christmases past and an inspiration for Christmases yet to be. My memories have come full circle, for this year I am the mother of two small children. This season, after I tie my apron strings, my son and I will sift through the multitude of Grandma's cutters so he can pick out his favorite. I hope that someday when they're all grown up they'll think as I do, and say, "My mom and I baked the BEST Christmas cookies IN THE WORLD!" Until then, I'll cherish my new memories in the making.

Rebecca Suiter
Checotah, OK

One of my favorite Christmases was the one I spent in Fairborn, Ohio in 1958 with my cousins and grandmother. It was the second Christmas we had spent in Ohio. The first time, my father had driven all night from our home in Oklahoma in a Buick convertible during a snowstorm. We were afraid if we stopped we would become stranded! My mother said afterward we wouldn't go to Ohio during Christmas again because of that hair-raising experience, but somehow the memories of the ordeal must have mellowed and she changed her mind. Luckily, the second time we went the weather was clear, and we enjoyed the beautiful snow that fell after we arrived. We were enjoying the hustle and bustle of making last-minute plans and sharing secrets with our cousins when my brother and I noticed that my aunt stayed in her bedroom quite a lot. We were told not to disturb her.

Christmas Eve came, and we all attended a beautiful midnight candlelight service. We then retired for the night, dreaming of the wonderful things Santa would bring. The next morning we awoke to find our first Christmas stockings hanging on the mantel! Mine was filled with chocolate coin candies, an orange, other Christmas candies and a small dime store porcelain Christmas angel figurine, which I still cherish to this day. My dad's family was German, and to them Christmas was the biggest event of the year. My mother's family was French, and they had never hung stockings on Christmas Eve. Mother said that soon after our arrival, my aunt had asked if we had stockings. Since we didn't, she purchased red and white flannel and made one for each of us, Mother and Dad included! So that was what Aunt Mildred was doing in her bedroom! Mother said that she and my aunt really enjoyed going downtown and purchasing the small items to put in the stockings.

After I married, my mother gave me the faded red flannel stocking with my name embroidered in green on its white cuff. I treasure it, and each time I look at it I think of that wonderful Christmas in Ohio. My daughter, my only child, has never been without a Christmas stocking. In fact for her first Christmas, when she was only two months old, I stayed up half the night before Christmas Eve making her a stocking...a store-bought one just wouldn't do!

7

Memories

Joan Brochu
Hardwick, VT

I remember the Christmases so vividly! It was high school years, 1949-1952. We all belonged to the C.Y.O. choir and so we would all go to midnight mass and sing the mass; then we would go to my husband's (then boyfriend's) house. He had eleven brothers and sisters and four or five of them sang in the choir also. We had so much fun! John's mother would fix a big meal and there were always meat pies "Tourtieres" which everyone waited for. (See recipe on p. 146.)

Then we would trim the tree; it was getting light out by this time. John would take me home in time for my family Christmas. I had six brothers and sisters, so we also had a great time. This tradition of going to John's parents' for Midnight Mass dinner had to stop when we came home from there one year, as our son was getting up for his presents and we had to play with him all day after "no sleep!" Those days will never be again; what a wonderful time in our lives.

Wendy Lee Paffenroth
Pine Island, NY

The first Christmas we had did not have a lot of decorations. My wise mother had been purchasing one special Christmas ornament a year for me and dating them. Since I was crazy about horses, many of my ornaments were rocking horses, stick horses, etc. These adorned my first "married" Christmas tree. I also purchased my first "gold" ornament and had the year and our names inscribed on it. Each year I add a new one to our tree. In October we will be married 19 years, but this is our 20th tree, so I will try to find something very special for it.

I also started a tradition of engraving ornaments for my son and daughter. They have one for each year, and when they move out I will present them with their special box of memories to hang on their tree.

Janet Obenchain
Roanoke, VA

My husband and I have a standing "date" on Christmas Eve that started 10 years ago when we were dating.

In our town, we have a fabulous city market with shops, restaurants and local farmers selling their wares. Every year my husband and I go down to the market to get away from all of the hustle and bustle that the holidays bring. We walk around the market area, browsing the stands and shops. Then we go to the coffee house for a cup of coffee and something sweet. After we have lingered around the market, we walk up a few blocks to a display of trees that have been decorated by local merchants. The monies raised from the admission are collected for local charities, and everyone votes for their favorite tree.

Although this tradition started some time ago, it is still so special to me because it lets my husband, me and the spirit of the holidays spend some time alone.

Karen Hoblak
West Mifflin, PA

We all look forward to gaily wrapped gifts under the Christmas tree, but quite often we find ourselves dreading the time-consuming process that creates those beautiful packages.

A few years ago, my daughter Kathy said, "Let's have a Christmas gift-wrapping party," and so began a lovely family tradition. About a week before Christmas my daughters and I gather at one of our homes with our gifts and wrapping supplies. We spread out on the floor for a marathon wrapping session. A warm and welcoming atmosphere has been created with glowing candles, a lighted Christmas tree and familiar carols playing in the background.

While we wrap gifts, someone reads an inspiring Christmas story. Eventually we stop for a snack and remember past Christmases as we look forward to those in the future.

After completing our own wrapping, we help each other. As the evening comes to a close, we're thankful for time together, a job completed and for turning a chore into a family tradition and Christmas memory.

Memories

Santa

In 1978 my husband died, leaving me with two young boys. Needless to say, that Christmas promised to be a very difficult one for us. I tried my best to do all the traditional things and to have the best possible Christmas for our family. On the day before Christmas, I came home to a quiet house and was very discouraged. I decided I would start the fireplace to make our house cheery and was lugging in some wood when a delivery man came to the door. He handed me a beautiful bright poinsettia, said "Merry Christmas" and left. I opened the card, thinking it was from my mom or sister. Instead, there was a card that said "Someone is thinking of you...Merry Christmas, Santa!"

Living in a small town, I know the local florist so I called and begged them to tell me who sent the plant. They finally did. Much to my surprise, it was someone I did not know terribly well (she knew my family), and someone I would never expect. Believe me when I say it brightened my Christmas tremendously! Every Christmas since then, I have sent one or two "Santa" plants. I send them to people who have lost someone and who are facing their first year alone. I always sign them "Santa," and have told the florist not to dare tell the person if they call. I think I convinced them...who knows if it is true...but I don't care, it does my heart good and I believe it brightens the day of the people I pick. Now, just because lots of my friends love your publications, please just print my name as "Santa."

Deb Weiser
Gooseberry Patch

Christmas is a very special time at our home. It starts the day after Thanksgiving with the whole family decorating the Christmas tree while we listen to Christmas music and sip hot cocoa.

We make it a family project to bake and ice Christmas cut-out sugar cookies. We gather around the kitchen table to see who can make the prettiest cookies and, of course, the silliest ones. This time together always brings a lot of laughs. I also make lots of different candies to share with family and friends. We'll pick an evening, grab a Christmas tin of candies and we're off for a drive to look at Christmas lights. We'll drive around neighborhoods and enjoy the bright lights and beautiful decorations. Each year we pick a different light display to visit, such as the Columbus Zoo or a State Park. We play Christmas music, sing and laugh. Each year we try to do something special with our kids; something they'll always remember. One year we made a gingerbread house together. Everyone helped, even Dad! My, it was a lot of work, but such fun and satisfaction. Of course we took pictures, then took the house to a family gathering for a centerpiece. We knew it as a big hit when everyone got their cameras out to take pictures. Another year we made cinnamon hearts, stars and gingerbread boy decorations. We used them to tie on gifts and decorated our tiny tree in the kitchen with them.

Before bedtime on Christmas Eve, we turn the lights off and gather around the lit Christmas tree, each with a candle in hand. One person lights their candle and we reflect on Jesus being the Light of the World, then that person tells what they are most thankful for this past year and lights the next person's candle. When we are all done sharing, we close in prayer and the kids open one small gift. My husband Bruce and I open each other's Christmas cards. What very special moments! Christmas morn, we open The Bible and read the true Christmas story of Jesus' birth; then open gifts. After a special candlelit dinner, it's off to Grandma and Grandpa's for more excitement!

Memories

Joanne Paul
Marissa, IL

It was Christmas Eve, 1941. While shopping for some last-minute gifts in the neighboring town, a little girl had seen and begged for a lovely, warm, furry brown hat with soft, satiny lining. Although she pleaded, she was firmly told that she could not possibly have that hat. So home they went, and the family dressed for the Christmas Eve Sunday School program at their church.

Later that night, when they came out of church, huge snowflakes were softly falling. There was a full moon that illuminated the beautiful white night; it was Christmas-card perfect.

At home, as she was hanging her stocking for Santa to fill, in utter amazement the little girl cried with delight! For there, under the Christmas tree, lay the warm, furry brown hat with the soft satiny lining! But, how? She never knew. Her daddy passed away at the age of 86 ten years ago, the "little girl" is now 65. That little girl was me!

Cindy McAllister
Sheridan, MI

Last Christmas, everyone where I work really got involved in the spirit of giving. Each department received a live Christmas tree and stand along with information about a family in need within our community. We decorated our trees, gathered canned goods, wrapped gifts for the family and provided all the trimmings for the trees. We even had a contest between all the departments for the best decorated tree!

A week before Christmas we distributed the trees, gifts and food to the families in need. It was a truly meaningful experience for all of us.

Valerie Goodwin
Olean, NY

It is an ancient Hungarian custom to offer the infant in the manger green sprouts of wheat. Plant the seeds on December 13th, St. Lucia's Day. Fill a 4-inch flower pot with soil. Spread and press seeds gently into the soil, being careful not to plant them too deep. Keep in moderate temperature and water daily. By Christmas you will have wheat for your manger. A great project for kids!

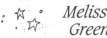
Melissa Shride
Greenville, SC

I remember, like many children, the incredible anticipation of Christmas morning. Upon awakening, the few minutes we waited for my parents to "clean up after Santa and his reindeer" were the most agonizing, but the most memorable. You see, while my parents put the finishing touches around the tree downstairs, my younger brother, older sister and I had to wait on the top stairs, where we could only listen to what Mom and Dad were doing.

We could hear Dad arranging boxes, bicycles, turning on the tree lights and Johnny Mathis warming up on the stereo. We could smell just the beginnings of Mom's orange glazed crescent rolls while we told jokes and stories from Christmas parties, whispered secrets about Mom and Dad's presents and shared "remember when" from other Christmases. We would quietly inch down the stairs until Dad would yell "OK, come on down!" At that point, it was each kid for himself as we dove into piles of packages studded with satin ribbons.

As a young adult starting my own family, I realize that my brother, sister and I shared more in those few minutes each Christmas than at any other time in our lives. I hope that my children will sit on the stairs of our house and create similar memories that will in turn teach them part of the true meaning of Christmas.

MeMories

Barb Agne
Gooseberry Patch

When my brothers, sister and I were growing up, whoever got up first on Christmas morning would wake up everyone else. We would always wash our faces and brush our teeth first because Grandma B. would always ask us if we did!

While we were waiting for the grownups to get up and ready, we would start on the top two steps of the stairs. Slowly we would move down a couple of stairs at a time because we would get anxious. Dad, in his dark maroon bathrobe, would go downstairs to see if Santa came. He would turn on lights and turn on the reel-to-reel music tape of "The Christmas Boys and Girls."

When everyone was ready, Mom or Dad would take our picture on the stairs. Then we could run down for our presents. When I got older I asked my dad for a copy of "The Christmas Boys and Girls" music. Now I play it for my children on Christmas morning.

When the Christmas season rolls around, I get out my music tape Dad made for me, and all the good Christmas memories of our family come back.

Crystal Parker
Gooseberry Patch

When remembering the Christmas season, I think about our unique family tradition. On Christmas Eve, like all children, we were too excited to wait for Christmas day to open our gifts. So our parents made a new tradition for our family. On Christmas Eve we would go to bed around 8 in the evening. We would fall fast asleep because we knew what surprises were in store for us!

Then at midnight our parents would come in to our rooms and wake us up. It was truly Christmas day...yea!! We would then open our gifts, have our holiday drinks, and of course take lots of pictures. These are some of the fondest memories I have of Christmas as a child.

Last year for Christmas, a close friend of my grandma's spent Christmas with us. Cliff was a gentle, kind, jolly old man (almost like the traditional Santa Claus we all know and love). When we began to open our gifts, my grandma decided to give Cliff a big surprise! She had bought an old Santa stocking cap for Cliff to wear. When she placed the old cap on his head we all began to laugh, he looked so sweet! Cliff loved our family very much, and wore that old hat with pride. Cliff passed away last year and we will miss him greatly this year, but that memory of him will last in our hearts even after the holiday season has passed.

Make some snowballs for indoors! Purchase white plastic foam balls in your choice of sizes. Push a toothpick halfway into the ball to use as a handle. Coat the ball with spray adhesive (be sure to protect work surface!) and then spray with a coat of aerosol snow. For extra sparkle, add a sprinkle of iridescent glitter before the snowball dries. Allow to dry overnight and display in an old wooden bowl or a tin pail by the fireplace.

Memories

Delores Hollenbeck
Omaha, NE

Our first Christmas while living in Germany was very unusual. We were living in temporary housing until our new house was ready, and we moved less than a week before Christmas, so locating a tree proved to be quite a feat.

The family who had previously lived in our house had discarded their tree, so I asked my two sons to bring the tree into the house. None of our four children were at all happy about the thought of a "used tree"! After the tree had been placed in the stand, all the family vanished. I put on the lights and garland and then called for everyone to come help decorate the tree.

Unwillingly, they began placing ornaments on the tree. In the midst of this we discovered a very tiny wooden chimney sweeper ornament that had been left on the tree. These are considered good luck in Germany. Before long this "discarded" tree was transformed into a lovely sight and stood proudly in the corner, the second time around. Not too bad for a "used tree"!

The next day we were given an invitation to join the 25 other Americans in our village to go Christmas caroling. This was the first time we had caroled in our tiny village, and what a great experience! We met at a little "gasthaus" and began walking up and down our little streets, carrying candles and singing on such a cold, windy, wintry evening. But soon some of the Germans came out, listened and ended up joining us in *Silent Night*. It truly was a wonderful evening...what a way to begin our holiday season so far away from home. We continued this caroling tradition for several years after.

For a beautiful effect, set lighted candles of different heights in front of a large mirror.

Sarah Dragotta
Doylestown, PA

Ever since our children were old enough to be read to, we have enjoyed collecting all of our books pertaining to the holidays, winter and Christmas, and keeping them grouped together in holiday baskets in the family room. We enjoy reading old favorites each year and adding new ones to our collection. When we tire of the stories, we put them in another part of the house, stored in the baskets and ready for next Christmas! We have been doing this with every season and holiday. It only takes a few moments to group them and keep the books nearby to be read and enjoyed.

Melinda Cato
Lake Jackson, TX

Take a picture of a favorite or special clock with the exact time your children wake up on Christmas morning. It's fun to see how the "wake-up" time changes with their ages. I use this for my first picture in my Christmas photo album every year!

Ruth and Stacey Tedrick
Gahanna, OH

One cold evening, my 8-year-old daughter Stacey and I went to the gas station. She loves to help me pump gas, so she got out of the car and put the charge card in the pump slot. She started getting cold, so she jumped back in the car. She saw that I was cold when I got back into the car she said, "I'll make you hot chocolate when you get home." When we did get home, I ran upstairs to change my clothes and when I returned there was a steaming cup of hot chocolate waiting just for me!

Memories

Wendy Posavec Gerbauer
Milwaukee, WI

During a wintry January afternoon, my Mother decided to spend her hibernation time cleaning out a box of ancient paperwork. When she's done this in the past, I've received immunization records and other medical documents, as Mom attempts to empty her attic and fill mine. So it was no surprise when an envelope arrived in the mail with a funny notation on the exterior flap that read, "You began wearing glasses on 11/27/62." (I was 4-1/2 at the time.) I chuckled with the thought that Mom was now sending me all of my records from the optician. I opened the envelope and, to my dismay, I held in my hand various sizes of scrap paper. The year was written at the top of each piece of paper and beneath the year was a list detailing each Christmas gift my parents purchased for me from the year I was born to present. Also included were letters I wrote to Santa as a child. My eyes filled with tears as I was in momentary shock at this simple but precious loving act of my mother who took the time to compile, preserve and share these lasting memories that have encompassed the past 38 years of my life. I thank God daily for the special relationship I share with my family. While miles may separate us now, our caring hearts will remain forever close! May those reading this story incorporate this idea among your holiday traditions. Your children will really appreciate this small but significant gesture in years to come!

Hang dainty tin molds on your small tree.

Christine A. Ziegler
Middlesex, NJ

When my daughter was in kindergarten, the school held a Christmas bazaar for the children to buy gifts. She was so excited to go Christmas shopping that day! She bought me two gifts, hid them in her room and couldn't wait to give them to me. On Christmas Eve morning her excitement got the best of her; she couldn't wait until that evening! We decided that we would exchange one special gift that morning and save the rest for Christmas Eve when we were with the rest of the family. Her gift to me was a small, gray felt mouse that I still treasure. To this day my daughter, who is now 19, and I still exchange one special gift on Christmas Eve morning, our special time together.

Kim Carpenter
Longmont, CO

It's very difficult to get everyone in my family together at Christmas, not to mention trying to fit family and in-laws into a very busy Christmas Eve and Day. So we came up with a great guilt-free alternative. Why not make Thanksgiving a two-day holiday reunion, complete with gift exchange?

Planning for this event begins in July with a name-draw; my mom and small children are exempt. We even had custom printed T-shirts made in honor of the event! As our guests arrive Thanksgiving morning, they are greeted with Christmas music, wonderful holiday scents and a tree awaiting trimming with our childhood ornaments. Our table is set with beautiful lace linens, gold-rimmed crystal goblets, my family's heirloom china and favors. After enjoying a traditional Thanksgiving meal, we adjourn to the gathering room for pictures and, finally, the gift exchange. We then eat dessert, and while the children are playing with their new toys, the adults partake in some lively games. After everyone has had their fill of dessert and laughter, we say goodnight. Those who don't sleep at our house meet at a quaint motel nearby. Friday morning, the dining table is transformed to serve a buffet-style breakfast of waffles, pancakes, French toast, muffins, breads, quiche, fruit and coffee. The morning is spent eating and enjoying the last few hours of each other's company. Everyone agrees that the holiday reunion gets better and better, and all the hugging and laughter is very therapeutic!

Memories

Kathy Boylea
Naples, FL

One favorite tradition is to clean out my daughter's closet. Being an only child, she has many things that are like new. We wrap these items and contact a local church who may know of a family in need. We arrange to meet the family at a nearby park and my daughter gives her wrapped presents to the children. I also prepare a basket of Christmas breads and homemade jams for the family. There's always a feeling of comfort when we go home.

Rebecca Suiter
Checotah, OK

One of my most cherished moments as a young mother was when my toddler daughter and I were passing the candy shelves in the grocery store. She spied the cinnamon red hot candies hanging in a cellophane bag on the shelf. We had always used them for the eyes, nose and buttons on our favorite gingerbread man. She exclaimed, "I want some gingerbread boy eyes! I want some gingerbread boy eyes!" From then on that is what she called them!

Start a holiday video library. The old classics are a treat for the kids on a snow day. Don't forget the popcorn!

Carol G. Aulabaugh
Janesville, WI

As a collector of **Gooseberry Patch** books, I have noticed and enjoyed the many anecdotes that you tuck in here and there as much as the many ideas and recipes your books have. Last year, a student of mine wrote "The Story of our Christmas Tree." It reads like this:

At my house we have a fake tree. We don't believe in killing trees for Christmas. We cut grapevines and we wrap them around our tree. My mom bought a grapevine star for the top of the tree. We have yellow lights on our tree that look like fireflies sitting on the branches. My mom filled glass balls with potpourri and hung them on the tree. We took old material and tied it on the tree. I asked my mom why we decorated our tree like this. She said that she wanted a "country Christmas."

Andrew Widner
Grade Three
Lincoln Elementary School
Janesville, WI

Instead of a wreath this year, tie a huge, fluffy bow to your front door!

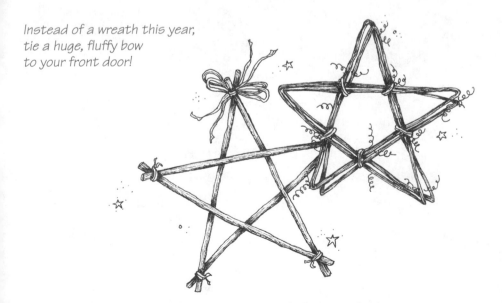

Sue MacIntire
Shoreham, VT

Since Christmas came on a weekend a couple of years ago, everyone in the family gathered in our 10-bedroom house in Vermont. On the afternoon of Christmas Eve, my daughter visited each guest room and swiped one sock per person out of their suitcase. That night we strung a clothesline from one end of the fireplace mantel to the other and hung the socks with clothespins. Small, inexpensive, but funny gifts were placed in each person's sock. For example, a picture of my sister wearing a baseball cap backwards and making a funny face was cut out of a group shot, put in a tiny frame, and tucked in her husband's sock! Christmas morning brought people downstairs with quizzical looks. For some reason, it didn't occur to this group of adults that Santa might have filled their socks!

Janet C. Myers
Reading, PA

Our three children have chosen or received a Christmas ornament each year since they were little. We've also saved the ornaments, everything from paper to dough, that they have made through the years in school or at home. Each year they enjoy rediscovering these ornaments as we decorate the Christmas tree.

This year there will be fewer ornaments on our tree. Our oldest son, recently married, will receive his boxes of ornaments as a gift. All those precious and wonderful memories will begin anew on his first Christmas tree.

Ann Glasscock
Alvaton, KY

Our church does something each year which I think is very special. On a night as close to Christmas as possible, a group of us meet at the church. We visit nursing homes and anyone in our community that needs cheering. We bring them a fruit basket and sing Christmas carols. It's a night of fun and fellowship that we all enjoy.

A
Sprinkle
Here,
A Sparkle
There

Easy Home Decorating Ideas

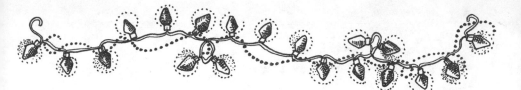

Recapture a Country Christmas

Cindy McAllister
Sheridan, MI

I love to make garlands to hang on cupboards, mirrors and archways, under shelves, in windows, on the tree and to give as gifts.

I use oranges, lemons and limes and cut the rinds into quarters and peel off carefully. Take tiny cookie cutters and cut out shapes. Use a toothpick to make holes in the tops of the shapes for hanging. Tie onto jute twine, hang up and let dry.

Decorating ideas are endless! String small jingle bells on red or green ribbon across your doors. Tiny cinnamon and applesauce ornaments hung from ribbons are pretty too.

Old chandeliers are pretty decorated with votive candles. Remove bulbs and all wiring first! Old bird cages can be decorated with real or artificial plants, flowers, tiny lights, potpourri in the bird feeders and life-like birds.

Hang mittens, stockings and hats on the tree, or popcorn balls wrapped in cellophane with red or green ribbon.

Make your tree a natural one! Decorate with pinecones, twig stars, found feathers, shells or dried flowers.

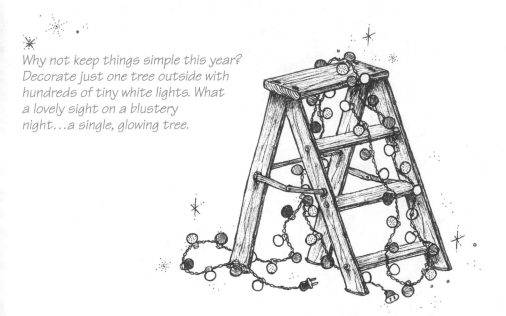

Why not keep things simple this year? Decorate just one tree outside with hundreds of tiny white lights. What a lovely sight on a blustery night...a single, glowing tree.

Decorating

Say Welcome

Judy Carter
Dunnellon, FL

Place hyacinth, crocus, or paperwhite bulbs in various containers. You can use terra cotta, tin boxes, ceramic planters or old canning jars filled with tiny rocks and tied with a raffia bow...beautiful!

Fill an old wooden bowl with cranberries, a crock with apples and artichokes, or put votives in goblets tied with bows or a basket of fruit.

Take a large cinnamon pillar candle, tie a raffia bow around the middle and slip dried lemon leaves and citrus slices under the bow.

Phyllis R. Stout
East Palatka, FL

Being a southern girl, I always decorate with our beautiful magnolia leaves during the holidays. I spray the leaves gold along with our southern long-needled pine pinecones. I then place them in a hunter green basket tied with gold and green wired ribbons and bows. So simple, but so elegant.

Thyra Zengel
Stockton, NJ

For decorating I take my old gourds from Halloween and Thanksgiving and spray paint them metallic gold or silver. I then place them in cut greens on my mantel and windowsills or in baskets with pinecones.

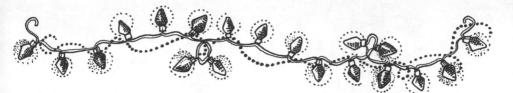

Great Flea Market Finds

Tami Bowman
Gooseberry Patch

☆ Old set of children's blocks. Great to spell out a seasonal welcome anytime of year! (Merry Christmas, Welcome, Happy Home.)

☆ A old chalkboard...wonderful for jotting down clever Christmas wishes (as well as notes and phone messages every day.)

☆ A pair of antique snow shoes...adds country charm to holiday decorating. Place them under the tree or beside the bed in the guest room.

☆ Old glass lanterns...add a touch of glowing candlelight to your mantel or holiday table.

☆ Aged wooden bowls...perfect for holding shiny red apples, snips of fresh greenery or several tiny presents.

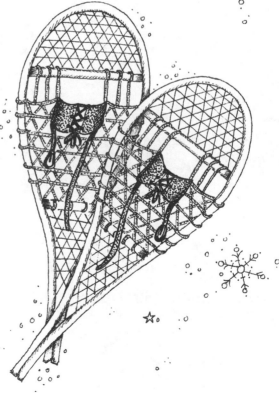

☆ Tiny vintage muffin tins...for holding white votive candles or yummy chocolate truffles.

Decorating

Comfort & Joy

Judy Hand
Centre Hall, PA

String up your favorite cookie cutters on Christmas ribbon or homespun ribbon, or make your own ribbon out of leftover fabric cut into scraps. I tie each cutter onto the main ribbon with a bow and drape the "garland of cutters" over my kitchen door frames and windows. I've even been known to add a few gingerbread or applesauce cookies made from each cutter shape; either alternating cookies and cutters, or sometimes attaching three cookies in the middle of the swag and some on the ends of the swag that hang down. It's inexpensive, fun and kids just love to help! They actually can do it all, and Mom can be working on other festive ideas. Go a step beyond and add greens and cinnamon sticks!

Amy Janac
Bryan, TX

My grandmother has always given the grandkids a Christmas ornament for Christmas. Needless to say, we have lots…and they don't all fit on the tree. So we've put them on a garland along the mantel with a little ribbon and lights. This way we use all our special ornaments!

Pat Husek
St. Joseph, MI

Keep a journal of what went "right" and "wrong" with food, decorations and gift giving. In my journal I describe the table linens and which dishes and accessories I used. Then, the following year, I try something entirely new or, if I'm in a hurry for an event, I can look at my journal and rely on what worked in past years.

You can also list guests' likes and dislikes, new ideas to try and what to plan ahead for. It's a great working plan book, and fun, too!

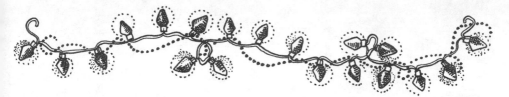

Welcome Home

Sally McArthur
Ostrander, OH

Let kids paint decorations on windows. Mix some poster paint with a drop of liquid dishwashing detergent. It can be washed off with window cleaner after the holidays.

If you're hosting overnight guests during the holidays, give their accommodations some thought. Even a little effort goes a long way in a spare room. Be sure there's a reading light next to the bed, or alongside an armchair.

Put a basket filled with often-forgotten things such as soap, shampoo, hairbrush, toothbrush and toothpaste.

For late night snackers, stock a tray with soda water, glasses, a jar of cookies and nuts.

Tune the radio to a station that plays music your guests will enjoy.

Have reading material; magazines, word search and crossword puzzles and a special Christmas book.

Make the room off-limits to kids and pets.

Put a vase filled with seasonal greens and berries or a bowl of red and green apples next to the bed.

Give guests a map of your city or town, as well as information about nearby places of interest.

A special treat for your holiday guests...leave personalized, beribboned ornaments on their pillows in the guest room.

A Cozy Bird Hideaway

Debbie Benjamin
Delaware, OH

After spending two to three weeks indoors with the perfect Christmas tree, you can extend its life even after the holidays are over.

After you have removed all the holiday ornaments, take the tree outdoors. If you were lucky enough to have a white Christmas, simply place the tree in a nearby snowbank. If there isn't any snow, use a large bucket or rock to prop up your tree.

Then, back in your kitchen, thread popcorn or dry cereal onto string to hang on your "Feed the Birds" tree. Pinecones covered with peanut butter and rolled in wild bird seed can be hung on your tree also. It will provide shelter and food from the weather during this difficult time of the year.

If you've used live greens for roping and wreaths, you can also place treats for the birds in these items. You can use wheat, dried flowers and other winter decorations to add to the beauty of this arrangement.

The satisfaction of feeding the birds will bring you much enjoyment long after the holidays are gone.

According to an old German legend, if you find a bird's nest in the tree that you harvest for Christmas, you will have an entire year of health and happiness!

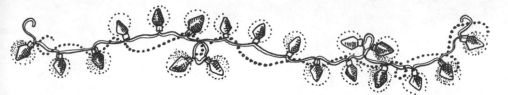

Just the Right Tree

Mary Murray
Gooseberry Patch

There are over a dozen different types of evergreens sold in the United States for use as Christmas trees! The most popular are the Douglas fir, balsam fir and Scotch pine. How do you find the one that's right for your family? Firs have a strong fragrance, and they, along with Scotch pine, are long-lasting. Both are good choices if you like to leave your tree up for a long time.

Scotch pine is hardy; even if you forget to water it, it rarely loses its needles. Blue spruce trees have sturdy branches for those sometimes heavy ornaments, but they're also the quickest type of tree to dry out.

Test your tree to see how fresh it is. Bounce it on the ground; if it's fresh you should lose very few needles. Another test is to pull the needles at the end of a branch. If they come out easily, the tree's already too dry, making it a bad candidate to bring into a heated house.

Some trees have been dyed to look fresher than they are. Look underneath the needles; there will be a difference in color if it's been dyed.

You might consider buying a live tree this year. Remember to dig the hole in preparation for replanting in October, before the ground freezes! When you bring your tree home, let the ball soak up as much water as it wants, then remove the burlap wrapping and let the excess water drain. Wrap the root ball in heavy plastic and secure tightly. You can buy an antidesiccant spray from a nursery and spray the branches; this will help prevent moisture loss. Remember, live trees can't be kept indoors for more than a week!

If you forgot to dig your hole before the ground was frozen, keep your tree in an unheated but sheltered place and cover the root ball with a blanket until you are ready to plant in the spring.

Decorating

Little Holiday Touches

Melissa Shride
Greenville, SC

Keep a wooden bowl or basket by the front door filled with little inexpensive or homemade ornaments. Give them to family and friends when they head for their own homes. These little tokens are also a nice surprise for people who deliver the mail or newspaper, read the meters or clean your house.

An interesting way to serve cold drinks at a party is to line your favorite basket with plastic and fill with crushed ice. This will keep miniature bottles of wine, soft drinks, or bottled water cold and at people's fingertips.

Wax seal the envelopes of your Christmas cards. Card and gift shops carry an assortment of designs that look striking with red, green or gold wax.

Beverly Botten
Silver Spring, MD

Once your children are old enough to come up with "wish lists" for Christmas, date them and file away after Santa has done his shopping. When your children are grown, they will enjoy looking over a piece of their past.

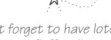

Don't forget to have lots of extra, fluffy pillows on hand for holiday guests (and little ones who want to snuggle!).

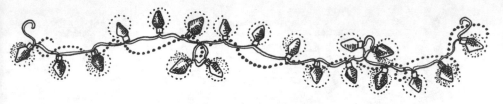

Winter Artist

Jack Frost with his pastry brush
Paints all the lawns and trees
Sparkles all the rooftops
And everything he sees.
Sometimes when I go outside
He decorates my head,
Sprinkles snowflakes
on my coat
and turns my nose to red.

Maxine Smith
Ogden, UT

Barbara Bargdill
Gooseberry Patch

Keep a small box in the garage filled with items needed to make a snowman. Hats, mittens and wooly scarves can be picked up for almost nothing at yard sales and flea markets during the summer months. Add some twigs and coal pieces or rocks and your kids are all ready for that "snow day" snowman. No more snowy boots in the house looking for snowman essentials!

Lori Jayne Bay
Delaware, OH

On snowy days when school is closed and your sanity is tested, bundle up the kids...arm them with spray bottles filled with tempura paint and water and design a snow mural in the drifts. When your masterpiece is complete, enjoy a cup of cocoa with peppermint candy cane stirrers!

There's No Place Like Home

Mary Murray
Gooseberry Patch

Decorate the outside of your home with special touches that reflect Colonial Williamsburg. Hang a lovely mixture of greens, holly berries, yarrow and lady apples on your garden gate or fence. Hang a swag of magnolia leaves, apples, pinecones, lemons, white pine and boxwood on your shutters or door.

Using a small planter filled with florist's foam securely fastened to your porch railing, create an open airy cascade of yarrow, pinecones, ivy, cedar and boxwood. A hanging cluster is also beautiful for porch railing. Apples of various sizes are wired together, then wired to a short piece of pine roping, holly branches and boxwood. Hang the cluster vertically using sprigs of holly to hide the wires and stem ends.

Overlapping magnolia leaves on the outer border and placing a large pineapple in the middle of a plywood plaque can make a dramatic doorway decoration. Outline the pineapple with red apples, nuts, and cranberries, a traditional symbol of hospitality!

Fill canning jars, old or new, with potpourri, pinecones, dried apple and orange slices. Leaving off the jar lid, insert a votive holder with a votive candle inside. The votive holder will sit just inside the jar rim without slipping inside. Top off the jar with a raffia or tartan bow tied around the jar neck. Beautiful grouped on a dry sink or old cupboard!

Fill a doll cradle with greenery, apples, oranges, cinnamon sticks and holly. A wonderful decoration for a child's room.

Decorate your porch with old crocks filled with greenery, then tie a beautiful festive bow around the crock.

Make a mitten wreath this year! Use outgrown mittens on a greenery wreath, add a big bow...charming!

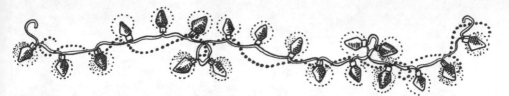

Sentimental Stockings

Judy Hand
Centre Hall, PA

For family members, I make Christmas stockings of "special and favorite things" that are associated with each person. For example, for my dad I sewed a favorite, outdated necktie down the front of the stocking, positioning the point at the bottom. I then attached a long ago Christmas present to him from me...a poodle tie tack (reminiscent of a family pet) to the tie. This serves a dual duty, that of securing the tie to the stocking, and bringing back a flood of memories! I used the narrow neck part of the tie around the very top edge of the stocking, and even had my husband tie the correct knot, then adjusted the pointed bottom to the desired position. You can secure the tie by machine or hand stitching, or fancy embroidered stitches if you have the time. Of course this has to be done prior to sewing the front and back of the stocking together...I always line my stockings because they are used each year and cherished by family members.

My husband's stocking is made from a wonderfully soft, warm and cuddly old worn sweatshirt, a favorite that he wore until it practically dropped off his body! Since he loves peanuts, I hand sewed peanuts, with shells, down the front.

My mother's stocking consists of remnants of laces and fabrics from favorite dresses, blouses and skirts, as well as special buttons. I made her stocking in the shape of an old shoe skate. The heel and toe of the skate blade are attached to the bottom of the stocking, but the blade hangs below the fabric and has a wonderful country curl at the end!

MAGICAL Crafts
HoLiDAY

Christmas Tree Topiaries

Cheryl Berry
Gainesville, FL

You'll need:

plastic foam cone
6 or 8-inch long dowel or twig
3 or 4-inch terra cotta pot
green sheet moss

florist's foam to fill pot
Spanish moss
desired decorations

Make these mini trees to place anywhere in your house! Cut foam to fit into and just below the inside rim of the terra cotta pot. Insert twig or dowel into the larger end of the cone, one or 2 inches deep, and then insert dowel into foam that's inside the pot. Glue green sheet moss to cover the cone, then add Spanish moss to hide the foam inside the pot. Add your favorite star decoration to the top.

Glue on fabric bows, wrapped candies, potpourri, buttons or rosebuds for added decoration. A great gift!

Winter Snowmen

Karen Perry
Fredericksburg, VA

These make wonderful gifts or ornaments and are so easy! Every year I have an ornament exchange party and we all make these. They can be dated, so each year we add one more to our snowman family.

papier maché	small branches
toothpicks, painted orange	homespun fabric
cloves	spray glaze

Mix papier maché according to directions. Using it as if it were clay, make three small balls and put them together. Use half of a toothpick for the nose, small branches for his arms, and cloves for buttons.

Let the snowman air dry on a paper plate for several days, then add eyes and mouth using a permanent marker. Spray with glaze and allow to dry, then tie on a homespun scarf.

You can also antique the snowman before you spray the glaze on. To do this, mix one part dark brown paint to 2 parts water. Apply the stain very lightly with a cotton swab, then spray with glaze.

This year, why not have a handmade Christmas? When you draw or exchange names, make a deal with everyone that all gifts must be made by hand. (Remember to plan early!) You'll be surprised at the clever (and sometimes comical) array of gifts! Save the money you'd normally spend to sponsor Christmas dinner for a family in need.

Dried Apple Slices

Mary Lou Traylor
Arlington, TN

8 to 10 apples
lemon juice
2 t. salt
6 t. cinnamon

2 t. allspice
1 t. cloves
2 t. arrow root powder

Soak apples in juice for 5 minutes, then pat dry. Place remaining ingredients in a large plastic storage bag. Add apple slices and shake to coat. Dry apples in a 150 to 200 degree oven for 6 hours. Remove from oven and lay on wax paper and turn daily until dry. Use in potpourri, wreaths or garlands.

Although most families decorate the public rooms in their home, a bedroom with special holiday decorations can be beautiful! A small, or even large tree could be tucked in a corner. Place holly or greens on the dresser, nightstand or window sill. Drape a garland around a four-poster bed and include tiny white lights. Stockings can be hung at the head or foot of the bed.

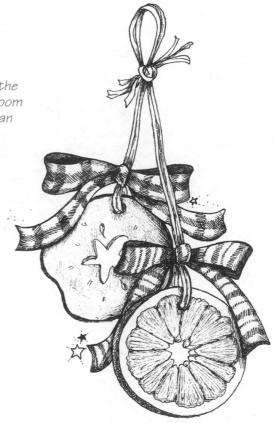

Crafts

Stained Glass Orange Slices

Denise Hindman
Titusville, NJ

Slice oranges 1/4-inch thick and dry on screens 3 to 4 days, or dry in an oven set at 150 degrees for 3 to 4 hours. When dry, string with ribbon, dot with whole star anise and juniper sprigs. Hang in a sunny window and they will glow like stained glass.

You can also put a few slices in a wooden bowl with pinecones and Christmas greens; lay slices over potpourri-filled bowls; hang on your tree or decorate wreaths.

Rosemary Reviver

Robin Reese
Fremont, OH

Combine one cup of fresh rosemary sprigs or 4 ounces of dried rosemary with two cups of water. Bring water to a boil for several minutes, then cool. Strain the rosemary sprigs and pour in a pretty jar or spray bottle. You can tie a ribbon around the neck for a great gift!

The bottle can be kept in the bathroom or bedroom. When you're feeling tired, splash some on. You'll feel refreshed!

Let your child design your holiday cards this year. Take a favorite piece of his or her "refrigerator art" to your local copy shop. Ask them to reduce the artwork to fit onto a folded sheet of paper, then copy the artwork onto a nice, heavy stock. Purchase envelopes to fit and send out as cards. Won't Grandma and Grandpa be proud!

Decorated Drawstring Bags

Rebecca Suiter
Checotah, OK

A nice gift to make for a child is a drawstring bag made of homespun and appliqued with a gingerbread man cut-out. Add other cut-outs such as stars, hearts and moons. Inside the bag put a book about the gingerbread boy, a gingerbread boy cookie cutter, other fun cutters, a small rolling pin, several cookie recipes, and cinnamon red hot candies for eyes, nose and buttons.

"Quilted" Christmas Bulbs

Kim Mariscotti
California, PA

These ornaments are so easy to make!

plastic foam balls, any size
fabric

small paring knife
ribbon

Cut a variety of fabrics in different patterns and finishes into 2-inch squares. Place the material on a foam ball and push the edges of the fabric into the ball with a paring knife. After the first piece of material is on the ball, place the second piece directly next to it and attach.

Continue until the ball is completely covered, then hot glue or pin a piece of ribbon on the top for your hanger.

These are really beautiful! So easy, but it will look like you spent hours!

Noodle Angels

Cheryl Berry
Gainesville, FL

These angels are easy for kids to make and nice gifts for teachers or family!

1/2-inch wooden bead
1 rigatoni noodle, uncooked
1 bow tie noodle, uncooked
2 macaroni noodles
orzo or egg pastini noodles, star
    noodles

spray paint, color of your choice
acrylic sealer
ribbon
paint marker

Glue wooden bead onto top of the rigatoni noodle; this is the angel's head. Glue bow tie noodle to the back of the rigatoni for the angel's wings and then glue the two macaroni noodles to the front of the rigatoni for the arms. Place glue on the wooden bead and roll the orzo or egg pastini noodles to make the angel's hair. When angel is dry and set, spray paint the color of your choice. To make this easier, place the angel on a craft stick and then place the stick in a piece of foam. Rotate the foam to evenly cover the angel with paint. Spray with sealer and when it's completely dry, use a paint marker to add her face.

You can glue dried flowers or a small ornament, to be held in her arms. Glue the ribbon to the top of your angel's head for hanging.

Use red and green spatterware plates to add fun to your holiday decorations!

42

Christmas Dough

Yvonne O'Keefe
Mesquite, TX

We have found something that entertains the kids and even Grandma on Christmas Eve Day. When everyone is restless while waiting on Santa, this dough saves the day! We make it in holiday colors and make Santas, snowmen and angels. The recipe calls for things you'll have on hand in the kitchen, easy!

1 c. all-purpose flour
2 t. cream of tartar
1/2 t. salt
1 c. water

1 T. vegetable oil
1 t. vanilla
food coloring

Combine all ingredients in a 1-1/2 quart saucepan over medium heat, stirring constantly for 4 minutes or until the mixture forms a ball. Remove dough from saucepan and let stand for 5 minutes. Knead dough about 45 seconds or until dough is smooth and well blended. Cool completely and store in an airtight container or zipper bag in the refrigerator.

Festive Fun With Cookie Cutters

Rebecca Suiter
Checotah, OK

Cookie cutters can be used for so many projects! Create appliqué designs for sweatshirts, T-shirts and children's clothes. Top crusts on pies can be cut with small cutters to permit steam to escape during baking and to make the pie look pretty. Small cookies can decorate iced cakes for birthdays and special occasions. Decorate your Christmas tree with cut-out cookies, or decorate a special tree for your kitchen or breakfast area with cookie cutters and kitchen gadgets. The possibilities are endless; just use your imagination.

The most obvious use of cookie cutters is making beautiful cut-out cookies. There is nothing like a plate of beautifully decorated cookies to highlight your Christmas table or to give to a special friend and, most of all, there is nothing like the cherished memory of making them with your children and grandchildren!

Gingerbread Cookie Tree

Martha Terrell
Dillwyn, VA

*Children will love being a part of making the cookies
and decorating the sugarplum tree!*

Make your favorite gingerbread cookie recipe and cut out into holiday shapes. Make a hole near the top and bake according to recipe directions.

Tie raffia through the hole and make a loop for hanging. Decorate your evergreen tree with tiny white lights, miniature candy canes on the branches and your homemade gingerbread cookies. A large cookie star makes a nice topper! Hang any extra cookies garland-style in a window.

Pre-schoolers love to play as if they're "big kids." Buy a brightly-colored zip-around school notebook and fill the rings with lined paper. In the pockets, tuck crayons, washable markers and stickers. They'll love practicing their letters and pretending to do their "homework."

Handmade Ornaments

Janet C. Myers
Reading, PA

*For the last 10 years I've made these ornaments with my 3-year-olds
at preschool. They're easy, and a real keepsake!*

2 c. table salt
2/3 c. water
food coloring

1 c. cornstarch
1/2 c. cold water
sequins, glitter, etc.

Mix salt and water in a saucepan and add a few drops of food coloring.
Stir until mixture is well heated, 3 to 4 minutes, then remove from heat.

Mix cornstarch with cold water and add to saucepan. Stir quickly until
the mixture is the consistency of stiff dough. If the mixture doesn't
thicken, reheat for one minute. Store dough in a plastic bag until
you're ready to use it. When you want to make ornaments, roll the
dough to 1/4-inch thickness and cut with Christmas cookie cutters. Put
a hole in the top of each ornament (with a straw) while it's still soft.
You can place a string or
cording through this for a
hanger. Decorate with
sequins or glitter, what-
ever you like! Allow
ornaments to air dry for
several days. Makes
approximately 18 4-inch
ornaments.

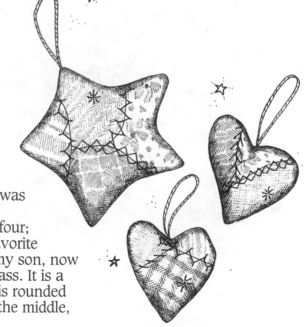

One of my most
precious ornaments is
a green Christmas tree
that had colored sequins
pressed into its dough. It was
made by my daughter at
preschool when she was four;
she's now 26! Another favorite
ornament was made by my son, now
16, in his kindergarten class. It is a
yellow dough star with his rounded
school picture glued into the middle,
surrounded by glitter.

45

Holiday Sweatshirt

Birdie J. Green
Nashville, TN

To make a cute holiday sweatshirt I place my tree cake pan on the front of a sweatshirt, trace around it and fill the pattern in with fabric paint. I then use my star cookie cutter for the top, trace and fill in with paint.

For ornaments I use buttons in heart, bow, star and animal shapes. Buttons can be found inexpensively, often with 4, 5 or 6 on a card. For extra strength, I stitch them on with embroidery floss.

I enjoy the fact that that it's completely washable and nothing has to be removed beforehand!

Dress up a keeping room or kitchen cupboard with children's toys, ornaments, wreaths, and votive candles. Use favorite collectibles, and greeting cards too!

Fingerprint Stationery

Dennise Heeren
Grand Rapids, MI

A quick and easy kids' craft idea that they can also give as a gift is what I call fingerprint stationery! All you need is four letter-sized envelopes, four pieces of 8-1/2"x11" white paper, an ink pad, colored pencils and magic markers.

Fold the paper in half widthwise. Then fold it again so it's greeting card size and fits into a lettered-size envelope. Cut off any excess paper if necessary.

Have the kids practice making their fingerprints on a separate piece of paper using the index finger and thumb...these work best. When you're ready to begin, make sure the card folds are at the top and left. Then let the kids dip their fingers in the ink pad and make their design! Birds, race cars, flowers...let them use their imagination!

To help keep the paper clean, the kids should wipe any excess ink from their fingers frequently to allow the prints to show clearly. Decorate with colored pencils, markers, etc. They can sign or initial their designs. Once the cards are dry, gather all the cards and envelopes and tie with a ribbon or put in a box to be wrapped. You could even make a tag for each stationery set that says "Fingerprint Stationery designed by" and fill in your child's name!

Simmering Pineapple Potpourri

Shannon Barnhart
Ashley, OH

1 qt. pineapple juice
1 qt. apple juice
1 qt. water
3 cinnamon sticks

16 cloves
2 T. allspice
3 T. pickling spice

Mix all ingredients together in a large saucepan. Bring to a boil, then reduce to a simmer. Continue to simmer for a wonderful holiday fragrance! Can also be heated in a slow cooker.

Wax Ornaments

Theresa Burkeland
Sun Prairie, WI

potpourri burner
scented potpourri wax
colored raffia
candy molds
medicine dropper

Begin by melting wax in a potpourri burner; set aside. Next, make the hanger by cutting raffia into 7-inch lengths and placing ends into the top of the candy mold. Being very careful, use the medicine dropper to slowly add the melted wax to the mold until filled. Place molds in freezer to harden and when completely cool and solid, ornament will easily pop out of mold.

Peel an orange in large slices, then push a mini cookie cutter into the peel. Let air dry, then add to your potpourri.

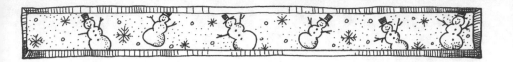

Pressed Cinnamon Ornaments

Theresa Burkeland
Sun Prairie, WI

1 c. ground cinnamon
1 c. water
candy molds

toothpicks
string, twine or raffia
1/4 c. additional cinnamon

In a medium bowl, combine cinnamon and water. Mix with a spoon until well blended. If too dry, add more water; if too wet, add more cinnamon.

Lightly dust the inside of each candy mold using the additional cinnamon. Pinch a piece of dough about the size of a grape and lightly dust with cinnamon. Press dough firmly into a fancy mold, wiping away excess dough from the back of the mold. Press the back of the mold firmly onto a cinnamon-sprinkled surface. This will help produce a good impression. Pop ornament out of mold. If too sticky, dust mold with more cinnamon. Use the toothpick to carefully make a hole for hanging. Place on a wire rack or cookie sheet, turning daily so they dry evenly, approximately 3 days. Insert twine, string, or raffia to hang.

Christmas Potpourri

Shannon Barnhart
Ashley, OH

1 qt. fir needles
1 c. dried mixed fruit, without membranes and thinly shredded
1 c. rosemary
1/2 c. basil
2 or 4 bay leaves, coarsely crumbled
2 c. coarse salt, not iodized

Break needles into small pieces and mix well with other ingredients. Pour into small calico bags and tie securely with matching ribbon. Yield: 5 cups.

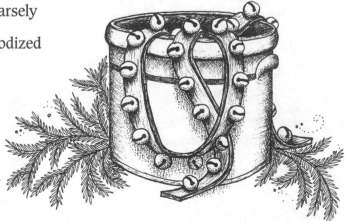

Sponge-Painted Stocking

Jo Ann

Use fun stencil designs to create a handmade stocking!

Supplies:

1/2 yd. muslin	stencils: stars, checkerboard, etc.
stocking pattern	acrylic paints
transfer paper	textile medium
disappearing marker	natural sponge
wax paper	plate
one-inch wide masking tape	paper towels

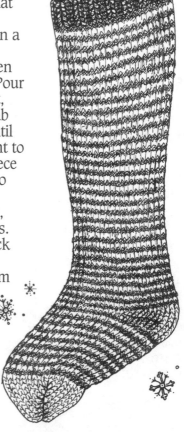

Machine-wash muslin and press while slightly damp. Pin fabric to pattern and trace front and back outlines with disappearing marker, then cut out. Place a length of wax paper on a flat surface. Lay fabric on wax paper and tape stencil firmly to fabric, keeping fabric flat. In a jar, combine paint with textile medium, following manufacturer's directions. Dampen sponge with water, squeezing out excess. Pour paint into a plate and dip sponge into paint, blotting excess on a paper towel. Gently dab paint onto fabric through stencil pattern until you achieve your desired result. Allow paint to dry before removing stencil. Cut a 3"x7" piece of muslin for a hanging loop, don't forget to stencil it to match! When stocking is thoroughly dry, press with iron to set paint, according to paint manufacturer's directions. With right sides together, stitch front to back on seam, leaving the top of the stocking open. Turn right side out and press top seam inside. With right sides together, fold hanging loop in half. Stitch long edges closed, trim seam, turn right side out and press. Pin loop inside stocking and hand-stitch around edges to secure.

Make it merry, Wrap it bright

Gifts from the kitchen

Herbal Vinegar

Merry Christmas Marmalade

Gifts
from your
Christmas Kitchen

Toffee Delight

Karen Zartman
Clyde, OH

Pack in your favorite old-fashioned tins.

1 c. margarine
1-1/3 c. sugar
1 T. light corn syrup

1/4 c. water
4-oz. bar milk chocolate
8-oz. pkg. pecans

Melt margarine in a heavy saucepan, adding sugar, corn syrup and water. Insert candy thermometer and cook, stirring often, until mixture reaches the hard crack stage (300 degrees). Pour into a buttered cookie sheet and cool completely. Melt chocolate bar and spread over top of toffee, then sprinkle with pecans. Chill until hard and break into pieces.

Honey-Glazed Snack Mix

Kathy Bolyea
Naples, FL

4 c. cereal squares
1-1/2 c. pretzel twists
1 c. pecan halves

1/3 c. margarine
1/4 c. honey

In a large bowl, combine first three ingredients. Over low heat, melt margarine with honey and pour over mix. Toss to coat. Spread on a cookie sheet and bake at 350 degrees for 15 minutes. Cool and spread on wax paper.

Microwave Peach Butter

Kathy Bolyea
Naples, FL

2 16-oz. cans peach halves,
   drained
3 T. powdered pectin

3/4 t. cinnamon
1/4 t. allspice
2-1/4 c. sugar

Purée peaches in a blender or food processor. In a 2-quart microwave-safe bowl, combine peaches, pectin, cinnamon and allspice, mixing well. Microwave on high for 6 minutes, stirring every 2 minutes. Add sugar and mix well. Microwave on high for 5 to 6 minutes, stirring once. Microwave one more minute, then ladle into 4 clean 8-ounce jars. Cool slightly, cover and refrigerate.

Quick Gifts

Deborah A. Peters
Breinigsville, PA

As a teacher, I often give "thank you" gifts to helpful students. I purchase holiday cookie cutters and make several batches of fudge in pans the depth of the cookie cutter. Using the cutters, I cut out fudge, leaving it inside the cutters. I then wrap these in transparent gift bags tied with a bag tie and some holiday ribbon. The center of the fudge can be decorated with a nut, cherry, or holiday peppermint.

For an easy, quick gift I keep colorful mugs on hand. I put excelsior in the bottom of the cup and then fill them with individually packaged gourmet hot chocolates or flavored teas. With the hot chocolate, I include plastic spoons I've dipped in chocolate to coat. These make delicious "stirrers." (See recipe on p. 62.) With the teas, I include spoons I've coated in a lollipop candy recipe. I wrap the package in tinted paper and tie with a holiday ribbon or raffia.

During the summer, you can make homemade bottles of flavored vinegars and keep them on hand for quick hostess gifts. Attach recipes for favorite vinaigrette dressings around the necks with strands of raffia, tied with a bow.

A cup of hot cocoa brings out the kid in all of us. Go ahead...treat yourself!

Cranberry Snow Candy

Juanita Williams
Jacksonville, OR

16-oz. pkg. white chocolate
   morsels

1-1/2 c. dried cranberries
1-1/2 c. walnuts, chopped

Melt the white chocolate in a double boiler. When melted, add cranberries and walnuts and drop by spoonfuls onto wax paper until set. Makes several dozen.

Pick an evening for a family "card party." Whip up some special snacks and spend the evening at the kitchen table signing your Christmas cards. Holiday greetings are cherished when they're signed by each family member. Don't forget pets! (Paw print rubber stamps work well for these autographs!) Keep one of your own signed Christmas cards each year in a holiday scrapbook...it's a joy to see the kids' signatures "grow up" over the years.

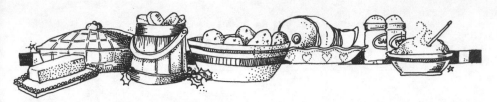

Lemon Scallion Vinegar

Judy Carter
Dunnellon, FL

A thoughtful hostess gift...just tie a raffia bow around the bottle!

1 qt. white wine vinegar
1 to 15 sprigs lemon thyme
peel of 1 lemon, cut into slices

4 cloves garlic, peeled
6 scallions

Gently stir together vinegar with remaining ingredients. Pour into a pretty glass bottle and seal with a cork. Let the flavors blend in a sunny spot for a few weeks.

Cranberry Lemon Vinegar

Judy Carter
Dunnellon, FL

Delicious on salads and in fish dishes.

1 qt. white wine vinegar
4 or 6 sprigs thyme

1/2 c. dried cranberries
peel of 1 lemon, cut into slices

Combine all ingredients into a glass bottle, cork and place in a sunny window for 2 to 3 weeks.

Christmas Kitchen

Hot Spiced Tea

Mary Lou Traylor
Arlington, TN

Make a double batch and share. So good, and good for you!

1/2 c. instant tea, with lemon   1 t. cloves, ground
2 c. powdered orange drink mix   2-1/2 c. sugar
1 t. cinnamon, ground

Combine all ingredients and store in an airtight container. To give as a gift, put mix in a decorative glass jar or old canning jar and tie a bow or string of raffia around the top. Don't forget to include the instructions: On cold winter nights, place 2 to 3 rounded teaspoons in a mug and add hot water.

Wrap your homemade canned preserves or salsa in festive tissue or cello bags tied with ribbons or raffia. Set them in a basket by the door and give to guests as they leave, or for that unexpected moment when a gift is needed. They make a pretty decoration, too!

Thoughtful Gifts

Tami Bowman
Gooseberry Patch

Share some holiday spirit with a busy family! Mix up your favorite batch of sugar cookie dough, roll into a log, chill and wrap in wax paper. Place in a basket filled with sprinkles, chocolate chips, gumdrops, some whimsical cookie cutters and baking instructions. Kids love the decorating, and Mom and Dad will appreciate your time-saving thoughtfulness. (Be sure to keep the dough refrigerated until ready to use!)

Make a special gift basket for a college student this Christmas! Include homemade canned sauces, pastas and wooden spoons in a colander for a clever (and useful) gift!

During the busy holiday season, send your neighbors an invitation to dinner (at their house!) Select a date and time and deliver a casserole fresh from your oven! Christmas cookies and some candles for the table will make it extra special.

Bake a batch of brightly-decorated cookies and share them with the cooks in your child's school cafeteria. They'll appreciate the treat from your kitchen!

Have your kids build a snowman at Grandma and Grandpa's house while they're out Christmas shopping. A thoughtful way to share some fun during the holidays.

59

Herbal Cheese Spread

Mary Murray
Gooseberry Patch

Pack this spread in crocks...the perfect gift.

2 8-oz. pkgs. cream cheese,
   softened
1/2 c. heavy cream
1 T. olive oil
2 cloves garlic, minced

3 T. parsley, minced
3 T. chives, chopped
salt & white pepper to taste
1/8 t. thyme

Combine cheese and cream, beating until fluffy. Add the remaining ingredients and stir until thoroughly mixed. Spoon into crocks or other small, decorative containers and cover. This can be stored in the refrigerator for approximately two weeks.

Christmas Crunch

Mary Lou Traylor
Arlington, TN

Layer in tins and it's ready for gift-giving!

12-oz. pkg. white chocolate
   morsels
1 c. small pretzels

1 c. apple-cinnamon cereal
1 c. graham cracker cereal
1 c. pecans

Melt morsels over low heat in a saucepan or in the microwave. Combine all other ingredients in a large bowl and pour melted morsels over mixture, stirring well to coat. Line cookie sheets with wax paper and spread mixture on cookie sheets and refrigerate. When completely cool, break into pieces and store in airtight containers.

Spicy Orange Butter

Kathy Williamson
Gooseberry Patch

A sweet gift for your hostess.

3/4 c. butter, softened
1/3 c. powdered sugar
3 T. light rum
rind of 1 small orange, grated

1 t. orange juice
1/4 t. ground ginger
1/4 t. ground cinnamon
1/8 t. grated nutmeg

Beat all ingredients together until smooth. Pack into small crocks or half-pint jars, cover and chill. When ready to give as a gift, cover the jar lid with a square of holiday fabric or homespun and tie with a ribbon or raffia. Tuck a note on the jar that the butter should be kept refrigerated until 15 minutes before serving.

Sugared Nuts

Mary Lou Traylor
Arlington, TN

Put in a pretty tin or glass jar and it's ready to give!

2/3 c. sugar
1 t. ground cinnamon
1/4 t. ground allspice

1/4 t. salt
1 c. pecan halves
1 c. whole almonds

Combine all ingredients in an 8-inch skillet over low heat. Stir constantly for about 20 minutes, or until sugar is melted and nuts are coated. Remove from heat and cool on wax paper. When completely cool, break apart and store at room temperature. Yield: 3 cups.

Thread a pretty button with wire and attach it to the center of the bow on your package.

Chocolate-Covered Spoons

Mary Lou Traylor
Arlington, TN

Tuck these in a basket with some cocoa mix...a terrific gift!

white or milk melting   plastic or stainless steel spoons
    chocolate
colored sugars

In a double boiler over low heat, melt chocolate in a saucepan. Dip heavy-duty plastic or stainless steel teaspoons in melted chocolate, coating bowls well. While still warm, dip bowl tips into colored sugars.

Allow to cool and harden completely on wax paper, then cover in plastic wrap and tie with a bow. A heart-warming gift tucked into a basket or a mug.

Fill an old-fashioned lunch box with home-baked goodies.

Chocolate Jar Cakes

Mary Murray
Gooseberry Patch

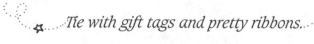

Tie with gift tags and pretty ribbons.

8 pint-sized wide-mouth
   canning jars
1 stick plus 3 T. unsalted butter
3 c. sugar
4 eggs
1 T. vanilla
2 c. applesauce, unsweetened

3 c. flour
3/4 c. unsweetened cocoa
   powder
1 t. baking soda
1/2 t. baking powder
1/8 t. salt

Prewash canning jars (be sure to use the kind that have no shoulders) in hot, soapy water. Rinse well, dry, and let them come to room temperature. Grease insides of jars well. Beat together butter and half of the sugar until fluffy. Add eggs and remaining sugar, vanilla and applesauce. Sift dry ingredients together and add to the applesauce mixture a little at a time; beat well after each addition.

Pour one cup of batter into each jar and carefully remove any batter from the rims. Place jars in a preheated 325 degree oven and bake for 40 minutes. While cakes are baking, bring a saucepan of water to a boil and carefully add jar lids. Remove pan from heat and keep lids hot until ready to use. When the cakes have finished baking, remove jars from oven. Make sure jar rims are clean. (If they're not, jars will not seal correctly.) Place lids on jars, and screw rings on tightly. Jars will seal as they cool. Cakes will slide right out when ready to serve.

Unsealed jars should be stored in the refrigerator and eaten within 2 weeks. Sealed jars may be stored with other canned flood or placed in a freezer. The cake is safe to eat as long as the jar remains vacuum sealed and free from mold. To enjoy the best flavor, try to eat all canned cakes within 6 months.

Almond Brittle

Pat Husek
St. Joseph, MI

Collect Christmas tins and fill 'em with almond brittle
for your friends!

1 c. slivered almonds
1/2 c. butter

1/2 c. sugar
1 T. light corn oil

Line a cake pan with foil, butter the foil and set aside. In a nonstick skillet, combine all ingredients until they come to a boil, about 5 to 6 minutes, stirring constantly. When mixture turns a golden brown and begins to stick together, pour into pan...work quickly! Spread evenly, cool and break into pieces.

Skip traditional gift wrap and make the container a part of the gift! Baskets, terra cotta pots, Shaker boxes, crocks, jars and tins make wonderful gifts in addition to what's tucked inside!

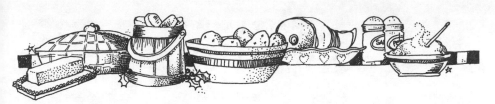

Christmas Meringues

Jo Baker
Litchfield , IL

A lovely, easy gift from your kitchen!

4 egg whites, room temperature
1-1/4 c. sugar
1/3 c. walnuts, coarsely chopped

1/3 c. dates, pitted and chopped
1/3 c. candied cherries, chopped

Preheat the oven to 300 degrees. In a large bowl, using an electric mixer, beat egg whites just until soft peaks form. Slowly raise beater and add sugar, two tablespoons at a time, beating well after each addition. Continue beating until stiff peaks form when the beater is slowly raised. Fold in remaining ingredients.

Drop mixture by teaspoonfuls, one inch apart on a lightly greased cookie sheet. Bake for 25 to 30 minutes, or just until faintly colored. Cool on wire rack, then store in an airtight container.

Vanilla Sugar

Mary Lou Traylor
Arlington, TN

A pretty gift to be used in coffee, teas and desserts!

2 c. granulated sugar

1 whole vanilla bean, split

When ready to give, place sugar in a glass jar with the vanilla bean. Allow flavors to blend at least one week. Decorate the jar lid with ribbon, fabric, or raffia.

Party Nuts

Molly Bordonaro
Worthington, OH

*Great to pack in a cork-topped glass canister and tie with
a fancy wired ribbon.*

1 T. ground cinnamon
1/2 t. ground ginger
1/2 t. ground nutmeg
1/16 t. ground red pepper flakes

3/4 c. sugar
1/4 c. butter
3 c. salted mixed nuts

Cover a jelly roll pan with wax paper; set aside. In a large mixing bowl combine cinnamon, ginger, nutmeg, red pepper flakes and sugar; set aside. In a medium skillet melt butter, stir in nuts, the remaining 1/2 cup of sugar and one teaspoon water. Cook and stir over medium heat until sugar melts and nuts start to brown, about 10 minutes. Stir nuts into spice mixture, tossing to coat; spread on prepared pan. Cool completely, then break into small pieces. Store in a tightly covered container at room temperature. Yield: 3 cups.

Buy rolls and rolls of beautifully patterned ribbons throughout the year when they're on sale. Tartan plaids, festive French-wired designs and shimmering metallics will dress your packages handsomely throughout the year, and especially at Christmas!

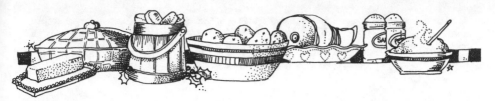

Gifts from the Heart

Kathy Doughty
Gooseberry Patch

Since my mother lives year 'round in Florida, Christmas for both of us is a little "blue." When I send her Christmas boxes I always include festive holiday napkins, cups and plates, and decorative candy and cookie tins filled with goodies. She gets such a thrill from these, it gives her no excuse not to entertain!

Jewell Wilson
Dahlgren, IL

When couples get married, a good gift is an assortment of Christmas lights, ornaments, decorations, and a copy of **Gooseberry Patch's Old-Fashioned Country Christmas!**

Wrap gifts well ahead of Christmas and pile them in brightly-colored arrangements in a basket, on a mantel, by the fireplace or on a table. Let the gifts decorate your home!

Great Stocking-Stuffers

Gail Renniger-Smith
Cortland, NY

- Fishing tackle for the fisherman
- Car wax and supplies for the auto buff
- Stationery, stamps and quarters for laundry for the college student
- Gardening books, magazines, gloves, seeds and tools for the gardener
- Unusual cookbooks, kitchen towels, spices and recipe cards for the chef

Look at garage sales, buy hat boxes and decorate them using buttons, fabric, paint or wallpaper to give to someone special. Put the gift inside and you have a real treasure!

Sally Borland
Port Gibson, NY

Make your own gift tags by cutting out paper shapes from cookie cutter tracings and decorate with glitter paints. Rubber stamps can be used too! Great project for the kids!

Theresa C. Hoffman
McComb, MS

I use this tip year 'round for myself, or as a terrific gift to a busy friend! When faced with the marathon baking sessions during the holidays, measure the dry ingredients for the recipes you'll be baking at the same time. I put the measured ingredients in zippered storage bags and label. It saves time getting the ingredients out and put back, clean up time of your measuring tools and makes the recipes almost as easy as a mix! If you're giving this as a gift, don't forget to include the recipe as well as instructions for adding wet ingredients.

Linda Gregory
Lakeland, FL

This is nice for Christmas or any occasion! It's like a gift basket with a tea time theme. Take any kind of tray or shallow basket and lay a piece of old linen, a doily or napkin on it. Add an old teacup, saucer and spoon. Then add any of the following: a tiny cream pitcher, flavored teas or coffees, scented candle or sachets, bath salts, fruit, candies or pastries, cassette of Christmas music and a handcrafted ornament.

Create A Memorable Gift

Crystal Parker
Gooseberry Patch

Always remember during Christmas that a homemade gift from the heart means more to someone than a present bought from the store.

Last year's gift was one of the best I could have ever given my grandma. Going through her photo albums, I came across old pictures of her family and borrowed them. I then bought a picture frame, the kind with the different-shaped openings, and beautifully arranged the pictures of her family. When my grandma unwrapped my gift she was pleasantly surprised to have received such a thoughtful gift made from the heart.

As a personal gift for a special person, I like to hand write a poem (written just for that person), and put it in an old picture frame. That person knows that they are dear in my heart when they receive a poem I wrote just for them.

I have a dear and wonderful friend who is a very talented artist. He has always dreamed of designing T-shirts with his own hand-drawn art designs. This gave me a great idea for a gift. I took some of his artwork and had a local shirt company make a T-shirt. I enclosed a poem I wrote, "Always Believe," so that he knew I believed in him and his dreams. This made Christmas special for both of us.

Thyra Zengel
Stockton, NJ

For a clever gift wrap, make rubber stamps from white rectangular erasers. Cut out festive shapes with a sharp craft knife and dip into cellulose sponges soaked in water-based craft paint.To get good stamp designs, the negative space needs to be cut deep enough to accentuate the shape, so cut the eraser design to 1/2-inch thickness. Stamp brown kraft paper in any pattern you like and when dry, wrap presents and finish off with a bow!

Wrap It In A Snap!

Crystal Parker
Gooseberry Patch

Here's a quick, easy, fun and inexpensive way to make your own gift wrap. Cut open brown paper grocery bags and wrap your gifts. Then use little colored sticker stars (gold, blue, green, red or silver), and decorate your gifts. Finish with pretty bows and ribbon. Everyone will love your creativity!

You will need:
scissors
brown paper lunch bag
cookie cutter, any size or shape
light colored tissue paper
school glue
pencil
stapler and staples
raffia

Trace a cookie cutter shape on the front of the bag. Then open the bag and poke a hole in the center of the design you just traced and cut out the cookie cutter shape. Cut out a square of tissue paper a little larger than your cookie cutter shape, and glue your tissue paper inside the paper bag behind the cut-out shape. It will look like stained glass! Put your gift in the bag.

Starting in the middle of the bag, make a crease and fold down. Then continue to fold the top part of your bag like an accordion or fan. After you have the bag folded, keep the folds flat as you staple the middle of the fold. Bring the sides of your folds together in the middle and staple the top of the bag where the folds come together. You'll have a little space between the two folds. Place raffia through the space and around the bottom of the bag. Then tie a big raffia bow and attach to the raffia around the bag. It's an elegant way to dress up any little gift!

Tuck bright red bittersweet and greenery in your open cupboard,
beautiful around salt-glazed pottery!
Add children's blocks to spell "Merry Christmas!"

Santa's On His Way

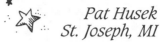

Pat Husek
St. Joseph, MI

A cute gift for a teenage or college girl is to crochet, knit, or purchase a washcloth of 100% cotton in a natural color. Wrap up a natural soap inside, wrap in brown paper and tie with a raffia bow. Terrific natural soaps are oatmeal, coconut, cucumber or almond. They also look great in a bathroom or a gift basket!

I enjoy stamping with rubber stamps, so an inexpensive gift that's enjoyable is to stamp a stack of gift tags, wrap with ribbon or raffia and tuck into a basket of goodies. I stamp with red, green, or blue ink on natural brown paper. A gift that's really useful!

A friend and I exchange gift bags of goodies each year. She gives me samples of her cooking; cookies, dried fruits and candy. I give her a sampler of my crafts; note cards, herb butter, teas, wreaths, or hand-crocheted items. These gifts don't cost a lot, and we really appreciate each other's talents.

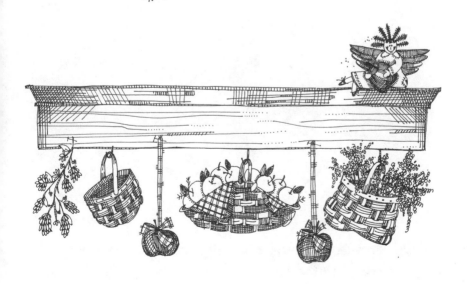

If you have ceiling beams in your kitchen lined with hanging baskets, suspend apples tied with green ribbon from the beams also...a wonderful Christmas welcome!

Make It Magic

Crystal Parker
Gooseberry Patch

For anyone who has little ones, turn off the television and give them rubber stamps, brown paper grocery bags and envelopes. Let their imaginations run wild! They can stamp your Christmas cards and make wonderful gift wrap. You will then be able to do other things on your busy holiday list, while your kids have fun with the stamps. What a treat for both of you!

It's difficult remembering to send a birthday card to those loved ones whose birthdays fall close to the holidays. I have an easy solution. Buy birthday cards in advance and always have them on hand. When you have a couple of spare moments, address, stamp and put signed cards in envelopes. Then have a folder that reads "December." At the beginning of the month, just put your cards in the mailbox to send out. This is so easy that I do it all year long. It saves a lot of time and worry!

Anytime you're not in the Christmas holiday mood, open up a box of Christmas lights and begin to decorate. It is amazing how a string of lights can lift your holiday spirit!

Ruth Tedrick
Gahanna, OH

Plain brown paper looks charming tied with ribbons, raffia, or decorated with buttons, pompoms, or pinecones.

Clara Hilton
Marengo, OH

Use new bath towels to wrap odd-size packages! Tie with brightly colored yarn, ribbon, or silk flowers. The towel becomes part of the gift and is a great "recycle" idea!

A feast
~ OF ~
time-
tested
Recipes

Christmas Morn Delights

Sausage & Egg Casserole

Janet Alvey
Mt. Washington, KY

Let breakfast bake while you're opening gifts!

6-oz. pkg. plain croutons
2 lbs. sausage, browned and
   drained
6 large eggs
2-1/2 c. milk

1 t. dry mustard
2 c. Cheddar cheese, grated
10 3/4-oz. can cream of
   mushroom soup

Grease a 13"x9"x2" casserole dish. Place croutons on the bottom of the pan, then top with sausage. Beat eggs, milk and dry mustard, pour over sausage. Cover with plastic wrap and refrigerate overnight. In the morning pre-heat oven to 300 degrees, remove plastic wrap and spread undiluted soup over casserole. Sprinkle with cheese and bake for one hour.

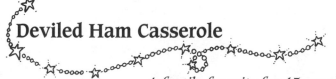

Deviled Ham Casserole

Patti Lusby
St. George, Utah

A family favorite for 45 years!

2 cans deviled ham
12 slices white bread, crusts
   removed
6 eggs

3 c. milk
Cheddar cheese, grated
1/2 stick butter

Spread deviled ham on bread, then cut in cubes. Put in a 13"x9" casserole dish. Beat together eggs and milk; pour over bread. Sprinkle cheese on top, cut butter into small pieces and put on top of cheese. Refrigerate overnight. In the morning, bake at 350 degrees for one hour until set. For the last 45 years this recipe has been our Christmas morning breakfast! My parents loved it when I was growing up, and now our grown children still consider it a special part of each Christmas morning.

Grandma's Coffee Cake

Terri Vanden Bosch
Rock Valley, IA

This was my grandmother's recipe which my mother made for breakfast every Saturday morning that I can remember. I make it many Sunday mornings because my family thinks they need a special breakfast before going to church. When my grandma died, my mother claimed her recipe books and found the original copy of the recipe that Grandma had torn out of a magazine. It was spattered and well-loved. My mom made copies of the recipe and laminated them as a gift for each of her five siblings; a present they all appreciated!

1/4 c. shortening	2 t. baking powder
1 c. sugar	1/2 c. milk
2 eggs	1-1/2 c. flour
1-1/2 t. almond flavoring	

Cream shortening and sugar well; add eggs, flavoring and baking powder. Add milk and flour a little at a time until smooth. Spread in a well-greased 11"x8" pan and cover with topping.

Topping:

1/3 c. sugar	3 t. cinnamon

Combine sugar and cinnamon and shake over the top of the unbaked cake. Bake at 350 degrees for 30 minutes or until a toothpick inserted into the middle comes out clean. Serve warm with butter on the top and a BIG glass of cold milk!

Christmas Kringle

Mari Thompson
Helsinki, Finland

We thank Mari for sending her recipe across the miles.

1 c. flour
1/2 c. butter
2 T. water
1 c. water
1/2 c. butter
1 t. almond extract

 1 c. flour
3 eggs
slivered almonds
1 c. powdered sugar

Mix first three ingredients together until mixture resembles pie crust; form a ball. Place in center of a cookie sheet and spread as thin as possible. In a saucepan bring water and butter to a boil. Add extract and flour, then mix in eggs, one at a time, mixing well. Spread over crust, almost to edges. Sprinkle with almonds and bake at 350 degrees for one hour. Combine last 2 ingredients for icing until consistency is thin but not runny, and drizzle on hot pastry. Serves 12.

This year, maybe Santa will leave a special treat for the kids. On Christmas Eve, hang a wreath of greens on your child's bedroom door. Decorate the wreath with tiny treasures...old tops, small Teddy bears, pretty pink ballet slippers...what a wonderful way for your child to greet Christmas day!

Breakfast Sausage & Fruit

Liz Plotnick
Gooseberry Patch

Try this idea with blueberries or pineapple.

5 7-oz. boxes beef sausage
   links, fully cooked
3 10-oz. cans sliced peaches,
   drained
1/3 c. maple syrup

1 t. nutmeg
ground cinnamon to taste
additional favorite fruits as
   desired

Brown the sausage links, drain grease, and cut into bite-sized pieces.
Add all remaining ingredients and keep warm in a crock pot. Serve
over pancakes, French toast or solo. Serves 6 to 8 as a solo dish.

*Windowsills, often too narrow to
support a vase, are the
perfect spots for
evergreen displays!*

Scottish Eggs

Kathy Williamson
Gooseberry Patch

A Scottish Christmas morn tradition. Very unique,
and a hit at the office!

2 eggs, beaten
1 T. Dijon mustard
2 c. bread crumbs

8 eggs, hard-boiled
1 lb. uncooked ground sausage
vegetable oil

Combine eggs and mustard in a bowl, mixing well. Place bread crumbs in a separate bowl. Using your hands, mold sausage around each of the hard-boiled eggs. Dip each sausage-covered egg in the egg and mustard mixture, then roll in bread crumbs. Repeat with remaining hard-boiled eggs. Refrigerate eggs from 3 hours to overnight. Heat 3 inches of oil in a deep fryer set at 375 degrees. Fry eggs, two at a time, until well browned, approximately 15 minutes or until sausage is thoroughly cooked. Remove eggs from the deep fryer and drain on paper towels. Cool eggs to room temperature and when ready to serve, cut into quarters and serve with Dijon mustard.

The perfect gift for the gourmet cook in your family...fill an oven mitt with tiny treats: whimsical cookie cutters, spices, spoons and favorite family recipes.

Cinnamon Spirals

Vickie

☆ *The scents of butter, brown sugar and cinnamon baking will fill your kitchen with delight.*

1 c. sour cream
2 T. shortening
3 T. sugar
1/8 t. soda
1 t. salt
1 egg

1 pkg. dry yeast
3 c. all-purpose flour
2 T. butter, softened
1/3 c. brown sugar
1 t. cinnamon
powdered sugar for icing

In a large saucepan bring the sour cream to a boil, then stir in shortening, sugar, soda and salt until well-blended. Cool mixture until warm and add egg and yeast, stirring until yeast is dissolved. Using a spoon, add flour to mixture. Turn dough out onto a lightly floured board and knead until a smooth ball forms. Cover with a damp cloth and allow to stand 5 minutes. In a small bowl combine butter, brown sugar and cinnamon; set aside. Roll dough to 1/4-inch thickness and shape into a rectangle approximately 14"x6". Spread the cinnamon mixture along half of the long side of the rectangle, then fold over other half. Cut dough into one-inch strips, then twist each piece several times. Place spirals on an ungreased baking sheet and let rise one hour. Bake in a 375 degree oven for approximately 15 minutes, remove from oven and drizzle with powdered sugar icing while warm.

Cut holes in apples or oranges just large enough to slip a tea light in. Smells wonderful!

Crunchy Apple Muffins

Crystal Parker
Gooseberry Patch

Try this recipe using the hybrid Jonagold apples.

Muffins:

1-1/2 c. flour, sifted
1/2 c. sugar
2 t. baking powder
1/2 t. salt
1/2 t. cinnamon

1/4 c. shortening
1 egg, slightly beaten
1/2 c. milk
1 c. apples, peeled and diced

Topping:

1/4 c. brown sugar, packed
1/4 c. walnuts, chopped

1/2 t. cinnamon

Sift flour, sugar, baking powder, salt and cinnamon in a large mixing
bowl. Cut in shortening until it resembles fine crumbs. In a separate
bowl combine egg and milk, then add to dry ingredients. Toss in
apples, stirring just until moist. Spoon batter into muffin tins, filling
two-thirds full. Sprinkle with topping and bake at 375 degrees for 25
minutes. Serve warm. Makes 12 servings.

*A simple arrangement of long-needle pine, old-fashioned tree ornaments and
cinnamon sticks looks beautiful set on a sideboard.*

Blueberry-Lemon Crepes

JoAnn

A refreshing winter breakfast!

Crepes:

1/2 c. biscuit mix
1 egg

6 T. milk

Filling:

3-oz. pkg. cream cheese,
   softened
1-1/2 c. half-and-half

1 T. lemon juice
3-3/4 oz. pkg. lemon instant
   pudding

Topping:

1 c. blueberry pie filling

Lightly grease a 6-inch skillet and heat until hot. Combine crepe ingredients and beat until smooth. Pour 2 tablespoons of batter into the skillet for each crepe. Rotating the skillet quickly, allow the batter to cover the bottom of the skillet. Cook each crepe until lightly brown, then take a spatula and, loosening the edges, turn crepe over, cooking only until golden. Stack crepes on a plate, placing a paper towel between each. Make filling by combining cheese, half-and-half, lemon juice and pudding, beating well on low speed for 2 minutes. Refrigerate filling for 30 minutes, then spoon 2 tablespoonfuls on each crepe and roll up. Top with remaining mixture and garnish with blueberry pie filling. Yields 6 servings.

Baked French Toast & Strawberries *Debbie Parker*
Gooseberry Patch

Try with soft Italian or egg bread.

2 large eggs
1/4 c. milk
1 t. vanilla extract
6 slices bread, slightly dry
3 T. butter
2 T. sugar

1/2 t. cinnamon
1 c. heavy cream, whipped or
   1 pint vanilla ice cream
3 c. strawberries, sliced and
   sweetened

In a medium bowl combine eggs, milk and vanilla, beating well.
Place bread slices in a shallow casserole and pour egg mixture on
bread. Allow to stand for 5 minutes, turn bread slices, and let stand
5 minutes more. Melt butter in a 13"x9"x2" baking pan in a 400
degree oven for 5 minutes. After bread has absorbed egg mixture,
place slices in baking pan and sprinkle with cinnamon and sugar.
Bake until golden brown, approximately 25 minutes. Serve with
whipped cream and strawberries.

For a thoughtful party favor, write guests' names on glass Christmas balls with a gold or silver glitter pen.

Cheese Danish Coffee Braid

Leigh Ann Ramey
Huber Heights, OH

This is a family favorite not only because it's a tradition, but because it tastes really wonderful! It's been a part of our Christmas ritual for 21 years.

Danish:

2 pkgs. yeast
1/2 c. warm water
6 T. sugar
1/2 lb. butter, softened

3 eggs
1 c. sour cream
5 c. sifted flour

Dissolve yeast completely in water, then add sugar and set aside. Cream together butter, eggs and sour cream. Alternating each, add flour and yeast mixture to the sour cream mixture. Combine thoroughly, cover and refrigerate overnight. The next morning, divide the dough into four sections for braiding. Roll each section into a 12"x9" rectangle and place on a greased baking sheet.

Cheese Filling:

3 8-oz. pkgs. cream cheese,
    softened
3 egg yolks

8 T. sugar
3 t. vanilla

Combine all ingredients and beat well with mixer. Spoon the filling into the center of the rectangle of dough and, using scissors or a sharp knife, cut the dough from the outside edge toward the filling into one-inch strips. Alternating one strip from each side, fold the strips at a criss-cross angle across the filling so it resembles a braid. Cover with a cloth and let rise in a warm place for about an hour. Bake at 350 for 20 to 25 minutes. Drizzle with glaze. Makes 4 braids.

Glaze:

2/3 c. powdered sugar
1 t. lemon juice

2 T. orange juice

Breakfast Cheesecake

Barbara Bargdill
Gooseberry Patch

Tastes like cheese Danish and is so easy to make!

2 8-oz. cans crescent roll dough
2 8-oz. pkgs. cream cheese
1-1/2 c. sugar, divided

1 large egg, separated
1 t. vanilla
1/2 c. nuts, chopped

Spread one can crescent roll dough in a 13"x9" pan, pressing the perforations together to seal. Combine the cream cheese, one cup of sugar, egg yolk and vanilla and spread on top of the rolls. Lay second can of dough on top of cheese mixture. Beat egg white and brush on top. Mix remaining sugar and nuts together and sprinkle on top. Bake at 350 degrees for 30 minutes.

A child's old red wagon makes the perfect holder for wrapped holiday gifts!

Christmas Tea Ring

Evonne Horn
Eyota, MN

A baker's crowning glory.

3/4 c. milk
1/2 c. sugar
2 t. salt
1/2 c. margarine
1/2 c. warm water (105-115 degrees)

2 pkgs. cake, active dry, or compressed yeast
1 egg
4 c. flour, unsifted

Scald milk, stir in sugar, salt and margarine; cook until lukewarm. Measure warm water into a large warm bowl and crumble in yeast, stirring until dissolved. Add lukewarm milk mixture, egg and half the flour, beat until smooth. Stir in remaining flour to make a stiff batter. Cover tightly and refrigerate at least 2 hours. Can be stored in the refrigerator for up to 3 days.

Filling:

1/4 c. margarine, melted
1-1/2 c. apples, chopped
1 c. sugar

1/2 c. pecans, chopped
2 t. cinnamon
1/2 c. raisins, optional

When ready to shape your tea ring, divide dough in half and roll each half into a 14"x7" oblong. Brush with margarine. Combine all remaining ingredients. Sprinkle over dough, then roll up long side and seal edges. Place sealed edges down in the shape of a circle on greased baking sheets. Seal ends firmly together. Using scissors, cut slices into the dough at one-inch intervals, turning each section on its side. Cover and let rise in a warm place until double in size, about an hour. Bake at 350 degrees 20 to 25 minutes. Frost while warm with 1/2 cup powdered sugar mixed with one teaspoon milk or fruit juice. Drizzle over top.

Christmas Almond Pound Cake

Wendy Lee Paffenroth
Pine Island, NY

Great for breakfast or dessert! Very special with vanilla ice cream or whipped cream. I first made this cake Christmas morning in 1976 and it has become a tradition to have while we open our presents! As much as we like this cake, I still only make it once a year.

1/2 c. margarine
1/2 c. butter
1 c. sugar
1 t. almond extract
1 t. vanilla extract
8-oz. can almond paste

3 large eggs
1/4 c. sour cream
1 t. baking powder
pinch salt
2-1/2 c. flour
1/2 or 3/4 c. milk

Blend margarine, butter and sugar together, then add almond and vanilla extracts and almond paste. Combine until thoroughly mixed. Add eggs and beat again, then add sour cream, baking powder and salt. Beat until smooth. Add flour and slowly add milk until mixture is thick, yet smooth. Pour mixture into a greased and floured tube or bundt pan, then bake at 350 degrees for 50 to 60 minutes or until the top springs back when lightly touched. Cool for one hour and transfer to a plate. When cool, sprinkle with powdered sugar. Also great with vanilla ice cream or whipped cream.

Using an apple stacker, build a pyramid of apples and pine sprigs topped with a beautiful pineapple. Stunning on an old cupboard!

Eggnog Quick Bread

Kathy Bolyea
Naples, FL

Mix up this quick treat for drop-in company!

2 eggs
1 c. sugar
1 c. dairy eggnog
1/2 c. margarine, melted
2 t. rum extract

1 t. vanilla
2-1/4 c. flour
2 t. baking powder
1/4 t. nutmeg

Beat eggs in a large bowl, then add next 5 ingredients, blending well. Add remaining ingredients and stir until just moist. Pour into a greased loaf pan and bake at 350 degrees for 45 to 50 minutes.

For a pretty, inexpensive table centerpiece, fill a large, clear glass container half-full with fresh cranberries. Use a tall round candle set in the middle of the berries and tuck in holly and greens around the base.

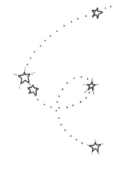

Olliebollen (Raisin Bread)

Sally Borland
Port Gibson, NY

A favorite Christmas morning tradition from our Dutch ancestors!

1 pkg. dry yeast
1 t. sugar
1/4 t. warm water
4-1/2 c. flour
1/4 c. sugar
1 t. salt

1/2 t. nutmeg
1-1/4 t. cinnamon
2 eggs, beaten
1 box raisins, seedless
1/2 qt. milk, scalded

Dissolve yeast with sugar and water, and let sit for about 10 minutes. In a large bowl, combine the remaining ingredients until blended well, then add yeast mixture. Let rise, uncovered, for one to two hours. Fry in deep fryer until golden brown. Serve warm with brown sugar or powdered sugar for dipping. Microwave to reheat.

Mom's Beautiful Babka

Melanie Elmore
Schenectady, NY

Before we opened our presents on Christmas morning, our family sat down to a delicious breakfast. Mom would set the kitchen table with red and green linen and we'd eat on special holiday dishes. Dad scrambled the eggs and Mom dished out her fresh fruit salad and sliced the Babka.

1/4 c. milk	1/4 c. sugar
1 pkg. yeast	3 eggs
1/4 c. very warm water	2-1/3 c. flour
1/4 c. margarine, softened	1/2 c. golden raisins

Preheat oven to 350 degrees. Scald milk; cool to lukewarm. In a large bowl, using an electric mixer, sprinkle the yeast over the very warm water. Stir to dissolve. Add milk, margarine, sugar, eggs and flour. Blend at low speed one minute, beat two minutes at medium speed. Cover and let rise in a warm place, free from draft, until bubbly; about one hour. Stir in raisins, mixing well. Turn into a greased and floured 2-quart tube pan. Let rise again, about 30 minutes. Bake at 350 degrees for 40 minutes, or until light golden brown. Let cool 5 to 10 minutes, remove to wire rack to cool completely.

Don't forget to decorate the barn or milk house! A gigantic wreath of greens with a red velvet bow says "welcome" throughout the holidays!

Raspberry Coffee Cake

Sara Grindle
Cordova, TN

You can make this recipe with blueberries,
peaches or cherries too.

10-oz. pkg. frozen raspberries,
    thawed and undrained
1 T. cornstarch
2-1/4 c. all-purpose flour
3/4 c. sugar

3/4 c. butter
1/2 t. baking soda
1/2 t. baking powder
3/4 c. buttermilk or sour milk
1 egg, slightly beaten

Filling:

In a small saucepan, combine raspberries and juice with cornstarch; mix well. Cook and stir until thick and bubbly. Cook one minute longer, then remove from heat; set aside.

Cake:

Combine flour and sugar; cut in butter until mixture resembles fine crumbs. Remove 1/2 cup and set aside. To the remainder of the flour mixture, add baking soda and baking powder. Combine buttermilk and egg; add to baking powder mixture. Stir to moisten, then spread two-thirds of the mixture over the bottom and halfway up the sides of a 10-inch greased quiche pan. Spread with raspberry filling. Spoon remaining batter in small mounds on top of filling. Sprinkle with reserved crumbs and bake at 350 degrees for 40 to 45 minutes or until done. Cool 15 minutes.

Apple Cream Cheese Coffee Cake

Linda Karner
Pisgah Forest, NC

2-1/2 c. flour
3/4 c. sugar
3/4 c. butter
1/2 t. baking powder
1/2 t. baking soda

1/4 t. salt
3/4 c. sour cream
1 egg
1 t. vanilla

Preheat oven to 350 degrees. Grease and flour a 9-inch springform pan. Combine flour and sugar in a large bowl. Using a pastry blender, cut in butter until mixture resembles coarse crumbs. Reserve one cup for topping. To the remaining crumb mixture, add baking powder, soda, salt, sour cream, egg and vanilla; blend well. Spread batter over the bottom and 2 inches up the side of a greased and floured 9-inch springform pan. The batter should be 1/4-inch thick on all sides. Add layers 1 and 2.

Layer #1:

8-oz. pkg. cream cheese
1/4 c. sugar
1 egg
1 T. lemon juice
1 t. vanilla

Layer #2:

1 c. apples, sliced
1/2 c. raisins
1 T. lemon juice
1/4 c. sugar
1 T. cinnamon

Prepare the first layer by combining all ingredients, blending well. Pour on top of batter. Combine all ingredients for second layer and carefully spoon over the cream cheese filling.

Topping:

1 c. reserved crumbs

1/2 c. nuts, chopped

Combine topping ingredients and sprinkle on top of cake. Bake at 350 degrees for 55 to 60 minutes. Cool 15 minutes and remove from pan. Serves 8 to 10.

Cheese Danish Pastries

Gen Hellums
Freer, TX

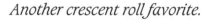

Another crescent roll favorite.

4 oz. cream cheese, softened
1/4 c. powdered sugar
1 egg yolk

1/2 t. lemon extract
8-oz. pkg. refrigerated
    crescent rolls

Preheat oven to 375 degrees. In a small bowl, beat cream cheese, powdered sugar, egg yolk and lemon extract with an electric mixer until well-blended. Unroll crescent roll dough on a lightly greased surface; firmly press dough perforations together to form a 14-1/2"x7-1/2" rectangle. Spread cream cheese mixture over dough to within 1/2 inch of the edges. Beginning at the long edge, roll up dough jelly roll-style. Using a serrated knife, cut into 3/4-inch slices. Place slices 2 inches apart on a lightly greased baking sheet. Bake 11 to 13 minutes or until lightly browned. Serve warm. Yield about 16 pastries.

Make a present of exotic coffee beans packed in a tin for a coffee lover.

Appetizers & Yuletide Beverages

Hot Candy Cane

Barbara Bargdill
Gooseberry Patch

What could be better after building a snowman?

6 c. milk, divided
8 1.5-oz. chocolate-covered
   peppermint patties, divided
1 c. white crème de cacao,
   divided (optional)

French vanilla ice cream
peppermint sticks

Pour 3 cups milk into a small saucepan. Cook over medium heat until heated through, but not boiling. Pour hot milk into blender. Add four peppermint patties; cover and process until smooth. Add 1/2 cup crème de cacao, if desired. Pour into mugs. Top with a scoop of ice cream and garnish with peppermint sticks. Repeat process with remaining ingredients. Makes 6 servings.

Purchase an old glass milk bottle at a flea market. Perfect for setting out once a year...for Santa's milk and cookies, of course!

Sausage Swirls

Melinda Cato
Lake Jackson, TX

Set out some pizza sauce for dipping.

8-oz. can crescent rolls
1 lb. sausage

1 c. colby or Cheddar cheese, grated

Preheat oven to 375 degrees and separate crescent rolls into rectangles. Spread a thin layer of uncooked sausage on each rectangle and top with 2 tablespoons of grated cheese. Roll from the short end and chill until firm. Slice each roll into 4 slices and place on an ungreased cookie sheet. Bake for 15 to 20 minutes or until golden brown. Serve hot. Yields 32 appetizers.

Holiday Cheese Bell

Mildred Rausch
Marysville, OH

Can be shaped into a Christmas tree, bell or ornament!

2 8-oz. pkgs. cream cheese
2 t. garlic salt

1/2 t. hot pepper sauce
1 T. horseradish

Combine all ingredients and shape into a bell. Decorate with sliced olives, pimento and parsley. Serve with crackers.

Pumpkin Dip

Melinda Cato
Lake Jackson, TX

Great served with gingersnaps!

4 c. powdered sugar, sifted
2 8-oz. pkgs. cream cheese,
   softened

1 can pumpkin pie filling
2 t. ground cinnamon
1 t. ground ginger

In a large bowl, combine sugar and cream cheese; beat until well-blended. Beat in remaining ingredients. Store in refrigerator until ready to serve.

Purchase fold-out pie crusts and cut fall shapes out of the dough. After baking, serve these with the dip along with some whipped topping ...little pumpkin pies!

Sausage Pizza Appetizer

Cassie Edenton
Nashville, TN

Try hot Italian sausage for this recipe.

1 lb. bulk sausage, hot or
   regular
4-oz. sharp Cheddar cheese,
   shredded
4-oz. mozzarella cheese,
   shredded

1/4 t. pepper, coarsely ground
1/4 t. oregano
dash garlic powder
dash salt
2/3 c. mayonnaise
48 slices cocktail rye bread

Brown crumbled sausage in a skillet over medium heat, drain fat and let sausage cool. In a medium bowl add all ingredients except bread. Stir until well-moistened and mixture holds together well. Add more mayonnaise if necessary. Cover and refrigerate overnight or until ready to use. To bake, preheat broiler. Spread one tablespoon of the sausage mixture on each slice of bread. Broil 6 inches from heat for 2 minutes or until bubbly. Makes 48 slices.

Crab Meltaways

Carol B. Johnson
Kinston, NC

Be sure to make plenty; they're delicious!

6-oz. can crabmeat
8 T. margarine
5-oz. jar sharp processed cheese
  food
1 T. mayonnaise

1/4 t. Worcestershire sauce
dash garlic salt
1 pkg. English muffins

Drain and rinse crabmeat in colander and blot dry with paper towels. Mix together margarine, cheese, mayonnaise, Worcestershire sauce and garlic salt. Fold in dry crabmeat, then spread mixture on split muffins. Quarter each muffin into four wedges and freeze. Keep frozen until ready to use. To serve, place under broiler until golden brown. Makes 24 appetizers.

Decorate the house in unexpected places...a golden ribbon around a stack of Shaker boxes...a garland around the hallway mirror, and even a bow or two on the backs of the dining room chairs.

BBQ Sausage Balls

Karen Zartman
Clyde, OH

A hit at your next party.

1 lb. ground sausage
1 egg, beaten

1/3 c. bread crumbs

Mix ingredients together and form into balls. Bake at 350 degrees for 30 minutes. This will make approximately 15 sausage balls, depending on the size. Cover with sauce.

Sauce:

1/2 c. catsup
2 T. vinegar

1 T. Worcestershire sauce
brown sugar to taste

Mix sauce ingredients together and pour over sausage balls. Place in a crockpot on low heat to keep warm.

Tie strings of thin red ribbon around the stems of shiny Granny Smith apples and stack them in a pretty wooden bowl or basket.

Salmon Party Log

Paula Braswell
Marietta, GA

This recipe can be made a day in advance!

16-oz. can salmon, bone &
   skin removed
8 oz. cream cheese, softened
1 T. lemon juice
1 t. horseradish

2 t. onions, grated
1/4 t. salt
1/4 t. Worcestershire sauce
1/2 c. pecans, chopped
3 T. parsley

Mix all ingredients thoroughly except pecans and parsley. Shape into a log or ball. Place pecans and parsley on wax paper, roll log in mixture and serve with crackers.

Tropical Chicken Wings

Lisa Card
Gardner, MA

A little different from the hot wings we usually have.

2 or 3 lbs. chicken wings, tips
   removed
10 oz. soy sauce
46 oz. pineapple juice

5 cloves garlic
1 or 2 t. ground ginger
1 c. brown sugar, packed

Parboil chicken for 20 minutes. Combine remaining ingredients in a large bowl, then add chicken. Cover and refrigerate for 2 to 3 days. Bake at 400 degrees for 5 minutes, turn wings and bake 5 minutes more. Discard marinade.

Give your favorite snacker a giant tin filled with peanuts, pretzels, chips or party mix. Decorate the outside of a large coffee can with acrylic paint in fun winter designs; snowmen, trees, stars, or angels. An irresistible treat!

Hot Pepper Dip

Deb Dye
Gooseberry Patch

Serve with chips or crackers.

16-oz. jar processed cheese
   spread
4-1/2 oz. can green chilis,
   chopped

10-3/4 oz. can golden
   mushroom soup
16-oz. Monterey Jack cheese
   with peppers

Gently heat all ingredients together. Serve with chips or crackers. Keep cheese dip warm by serving it in a crock pot or fondue pot.

No-Fat Bean & Salsa Dip

Kathleen K. Clarke
Portland, ME

Serve with tortilla chips or pretzel chips.

16-oz. can kidney beans
16-oz. jar thick and chunky
   picante sauce
garlic powder to taste

1 bunch green onions, chopped
8 oz. no-fat sour cream
tomatoes or black olives for
   toppings

Mash kidney beans in a bowl, add picante sauce and mix well. Add garlic powder to taste. Add green onions, reserving some for garnish. Place mixture in a bowl and cover with a layer of sour cream. Add any toppings you desire.

Barb's Crab Canapes

Sara Grindle
Cordova, TN

Also great with green olives.

3-oz. pkg. cream cheese, softened
1/4 c. feta cheese, crumbled
1 c. mayonnaise
1 c. Cheddar cheese, shredded
6-oz. can crabmeat

1 clove garlic, minced
1/4 t. cayenne pepper
1 pkg. English muffins
black olives, sliced

Combine first 7 ingredients in a medium bowl until well blended. Spread over English muffin halves, then quarter each half and garnish each appetizer with an olive slice. Broil for 2 to 3 minutes, until cheese is bubbly.

Sew jingle bells and tassels onto plain red napkins to add some merry music to your meals!

Mary's Reuben Dip

Sara Grindle
Cordova, TN

A great sandwich filling, too.

3 3-oz. pkgs. corned beef, chopped
16-oz. can sauerkraut, drained

8 oz. Swiss cheese, grated
1 c. Thousand Island dressing

Layer above in a quiche dish and bake at 350 degrees for 30 minutes. Serve with party rye slices or pumpernickel. Serves 10 to12.

Chicken Gemmies

Michelle Grippa
Aliquippa, PA

Make these when you're expecting a crowd!

12 chicken thighs, boned and skinned
2 c. seasoned, dry bread crumbs
1/2 c. Parmesan cheese, grated

1 t. salt
1 t. onion powder
1/4 t. cayenne pepper
2 sticks butter, melted

Preheat oven to 375 degrees. Cut chicken into one-inch cubes. Mix together crumbs, cheese, salt, onion powder and cayenne. Dip chicken in melted butter; roll in bread crumb mixture and place on ungreased cookie sheets. Refrigerate until ready to cook (up to 24 hours). Bake 20 minutes; turn halfway through.

Sweet & Sour Meatballs

Deberah Green
Gooseberry Patch

The current jelly adds a tangy flavor.

1 lb. ground beef
1 c. bread crumbs
1 egg
2 T. onion, chopped
2 T. milk

1 clove garlic, chopped
salt & pepper
2/3 c. chili sauce
2/3 c. red current jelly

Mix first 7 ingredients together, form meatballs. Brown on all sides. When browned, pour chili sauce and jelly over. Let simmer 40 minutes on low.

Shrimp Dip

Vickie

Here's a recipe our family loves! Easy and oh-so-good!

1 lb. processed cheese
1 lb. unsalted butter

1 lb. mini shrimp, cleaned and cooked

Heat cheese and butter in a double boiler until melted, then add shrimp. Once you do this, the cheese and butter mixture will blend together. Have a basket of crackers nearby for dipping!

Hot Christmas Punch

Jo Baker
Litchfield, IL

Float orange slices on top for a pretty garnish.

1 qt. grape juice
1 c. orange juice
1/2 c. lemon juice

1 c. pineapple juice
1 qt. boiling water
sugar to taste

Mix juices, water, sugar and heat thoroughly. Serve with cinnamon stick stirrers.

Use star-shaped cookie cutters to cut slices of lemons, limes, oranges and kiwi fruit into the shapes of stars; then float them in your holiday punch.

Celebration Punch

JoAnn

Refreshing any time of the year.

2 12-oz. cans frozen lemonade
   concentrate
2 12-oz. cans frozen pineapple
   juice concentrate
1 qt. water
1 liter ginger ale

1 liter sparkling water
1 bottle sparkling white
   grape juice
fresh strawberries
mint leaves

Mix all juices and water together in a large punch bowl. Before serving, add ginger ale, sparkling water and sparkling white grape juice. Stir to blend flavors. Garnish glasses with fresh strawberries and a mint sprig. Yield: 50 1/2-cup servings.

Apple & Pear-Shaped Cheese Balls

Martha Terrell
Dillwyn, VA

An elegant addition to any holiday party!

1/4 lb. blue cheese, crumbled
2 5-oz. jars pasteurized
    processed sharp American
    cheese spread
2 3-oz. pkgs. cream cheese,
    softened

1 t. Worcestershire sauce
paprika
1/3 c. Parmesan cheese, grated
4 drops yellow food coloring
cinnamon stick
lemon leaves

Mix blue cheese, cheese spread, cream cheese and Worcestershire sauce in a medium bowl with a fork until blended. Cover and chill at least 8 hours. Divide cheese mixture in half. Shape one half into a ball and place on wax paper. Sprinkle another piece of wax paper with paprika, roll cheese ball in paprika until thoroughly coated. Mold into an apple shape. Shape the remaining cheese mixture into a ball. Combine Parmesan cheese and food coloring in a covered container or large plastic resealable bag and add cheese ball. Roll cheeseball in Parmesan cheese mixture until thoroughly coated. Mold into a pear shape. Make a small depression in the top of each cheeseball for stem ends; insert piece of cinnamon stick into depressions. Insert leaves into tops of cheeseballs. Each cheeseball serves 12.

If you have a fireplace, have an intimate holiday dinner. Pull your table and chairs right up next to the fireplace. Keep decorations simple and open a gift or two after dinner as an extra treat.

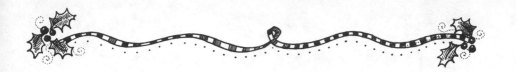

Christmas Wreath Punch

Jo Baker
Litchfield, Il.

A light, refreshing change!

3 6-oz. cans frozen orange juice 1/8 c. lime juice
   concentrate, undiluted 1-1/2 qts. ginger ale
3/4 c. light corn syrup

Combine orange juice, corn syrup and lime juice, mixing thoroughly.
Just before serving, add ginger ale and ice ring.

Ice Ring:

3-cup mold red and green maraschino
orange wedges   cherries

Fill the mold two-thirds full with water; freeze. Alternate orange
wedges, peel side down, with three cherries in each grouping. Add a
thin layer of water and freeze an additional 30 minutes or until fruit is
firmly in place. Slowly add more water to top edge of mold and freeze
until solid. To unmold, run warm water on the sides of the mold.

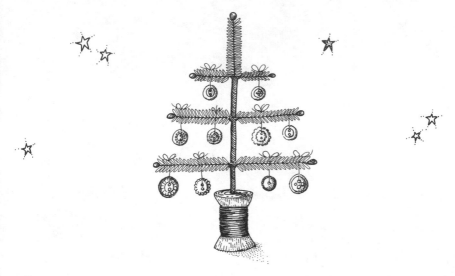

*Decorate a tiny artificial tree with old buttons. Tie them on with embroidery
floss. Wrap the base of the tree in a piece of homespun and tie with jute.
Perfect for the sewing room!*

Ranch Potato Skins

Kim Schaffert
Aurora, NE

*Add your favorite toppings to this recipe...bacon bits,
chopped tomatoes or sweet purple onion.*

4 baked potatoes, halved 1-oz. packet ranch dressing mix
1/4 c. sour cream   Cheddar cheese, shredded

Scoop out potatoes and combine cooked potatoes with sour cream and
dressing mix. Fill potato skins with this mixture and sprinkle with
Cheddar cheese. Bake in an 8"x8" dish for 12 to15 minutes at 375
degrees.

Brandy Cider Tea

Pat Husek
St. Joseph, MI

Fortify yourself with this delicious drink before you go out caroling.

2 c. freshly-brewed strong tea   1-1/4 c. fresh orange juice
1/3 c. sugar   1/2 c. brandy
4 c. apple cider, heated   1 lemon, sliced

Heat all ingredients together until sugar is completely dissolved. Serve
immediately or keep warm in a carafe. Makes 4 cups.

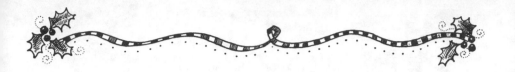

Holiday Grog

Wendy Lee Paffenroth
Pine Island, NY

Warms you to your toes!

1 can frozen apple juice
   concentrate
equal amounts of cranberry juice
2 oranges, sliced and studded
   with cloves

sprinkle of cinnamon
sprinkle of nutmeg

Prepare apple juice according to package directions using water or apple cider. Put all ingredients in a crock pot or heat on the stove over medium until hot. Ladle into mugs and stir with a cinnamon stick.

COZY!

Forcing branches to bloom in winter is a wonderful off-season pleasure for gardeners. After a long winter's nap, the buds are ready to grow when warmth and moisture are supplied. Just about any shrub that leafs out in early spring can be forced indoors; pussy willows, pink-flowering almond, wild plum, or bittersweet. A great way for gardeners to satisfy the soul.

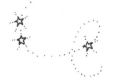

Appetizers & Beverages

Sparkling Punch

Kathy Bolyea
Naples, FL

A tangy, bubbly treat!

3 T. sugar
12 whole allspice
3 short cinnamon sticks

8 c. cranberry juice
3 bottles pink champagne or
ginger ale

In a saucepan over high heat combine sugar, allspice, cinnamon and 2 cups cranberry juice. Reduce heat to low, cover and simmer 10 minutes. Cool and refrigerate. In pitcher or punch bowl, strain cranberry mixture discarding spices. Add remaining cranberry juice and champagne. Serve at once. Yield 16 cups.

Glöggi

Mari Thompson
Helsinki, Finland

A Finnish holiday tradition.

1 bottle dry red wine
1 c. Madeira wine
1 T. ground cardamom
1 cinnamon stick

rind of 1/2 lemon
1/4 c. brown sugar
1/4 c. whole blanched almonds
1/2 c. raisins

Combine red wine and madeira in a saucepan. Add spices and bring to a simmer over low heat. Add lemon rind and sugar. Stir to dissolve the sugar, then strain to remove spices. Divide raisins and almonds into serving cups. Pour wine over raisins and almonds and serve in mugs or glasses with a spoon. Very warm and yummy!

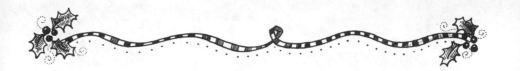

Shrimp Louis

Susan Taylor
Beaver Falls, PA

Make it the night before your party!

1 lb. shrimp	8 oz. cream cheese, softened
1 c. celery, chopped	1/2 c. mayonnaise
1 small onion, finely diced	juice of 1 lemon

Cook and clean shrimp, then cut into small pieces. Combine with celery and onion. In a separate bowl, combine cream cheese, mayonannise and lemon juice. Combine with shrimp mixture and chill. Serve with crackers. This recipe is best if the flavors are allowed to combine at least 8 hours.

Feeling stressed? Instead of full-course, sit-down dinners, plan informal get-togethers. Buffets are easy to plan; let everyone bring a favorite dish.

Rosy Mulled Cider

Deborah Donovan
Boise, ID

Warm and spicy!

2 qts. apple juice
1 c. orange juice

1/4 c. cinnamon candies
12 whole cloves

Combine all ingredients and heat to near boiling. Strain out cloves and serve hot with an orange slice for garnish.

Use your best tea cups and saucers for serving your holiday tea and cider.

Coffee Punch

Tom Huston
Oil City, PA

A sweet way to enjoy your coffee!

1 qt. coffee
1 qt. chocolate ice cream
1 qt. vanilla ice cream
1/4 t. almond extract

1 c. whipping cream
1/2 c. sugar
1/4 t. salt
1/2 t. nutmeg, grated

Mix together the coffee, ice creams and almond extract. Whip cream with sugar and salt. Fold into first mixture and sprinkle with nutmeg.

Hot Crab Dip

Lesli Jo Krieger
Deer Park, WA

Try a basket of baked pita chips with this.

1/2 lb. fresh crab, shelled
2 8-oz. pkgs. cream cheese
1 small onion, grated
1 T. horseradish sauce
2 T. cream

2 shakes hot pepper sauce
1/2 t. garlic powder
1/2 t. white pepper, ground
1 t. salt

Mix all together and place in a fondue pot or heat in a 350 degree oven for 20 minutes, or until heated thoroughly.

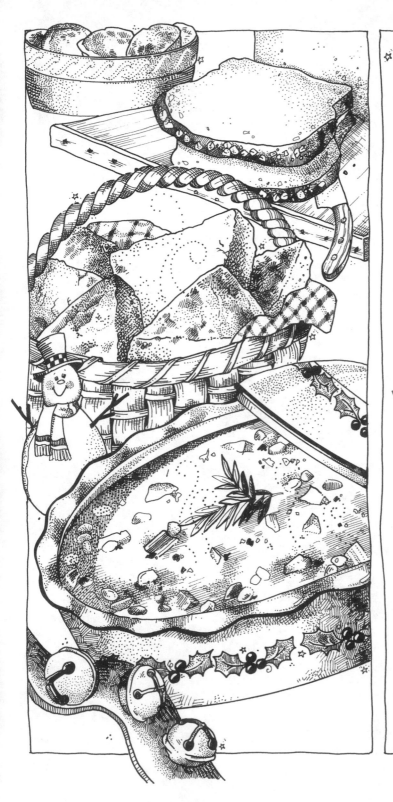

Soups and Breads

Woodland Altars Whole Wheat Bread

Carol Bull
Gooseberry Patch

My husband and I met at Woodland Altars Camp over 16 years ago. We fell in love with each other and this wonderful hearty bread!

1 T. yeast
1/4 c. warm water
2 c. hot water
1/4 c. honey

2 t. salt
3 T. oil
3 or 4 c. whole wheat flour

Soften yeast in 1/4 cup of warm water. In another bowl, combine hot water, honey, salt and oil. Stir in 3 cups of whole wheat flour, mix well. Stir in yeast mixture. Add more flour, 1/2 cup at at time to make a fairly stiff dough. Sprinkle a little flour on a board, knead 10 minutes. Shape dough into a ball, put in greased bowl and grease top of dough. Let rise 1-1/2 hours or until doubled in size. Punch down, divide in half, knead a little. Shape loaves into balls, let rest 10 minutes. Shape dough into loaves and place on greased cookie sheet or place in greased loaf pans. Split top, drizzle with melted butter. Let rise until doubled, 1-1/2 hours. Bake for 45 minutes at 350 degrees. Yield: 2 loaves. Excellent served with a spinach salad and white wine.

Broccoli Cheese Soup

Ruth Ann Geiger
Marysville, OH

A sprinkle of dill makes a tasty garnish.

12 oz. chicken broth
1 c. water
1/4 c. carrots, chopped

1/4 c. onion, chopped
1/4 c. celery, chopped
10 oz. broccoli flowerets

Combine all soup ingredients and simmer for 15 to 20 minutes while preparing cheese sauce.

Cheese Sauce:

8 T. butter, melted
8 T. flour

4 c. milk
2 c. Cheddar cheese, grated

Combine first three ingredients. When thick and bubbly, add cheese. Combine cheese sauce with vegetable mixture and serve.

Do you have a child returning home for the holidays?
Give her a rousing welcome by decorating her bedroom
with twinkly colored lights!

Savory Mini-Bagels

Barb Bargdill
Gooseberry Patch

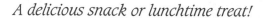

A delicious snack or lunchtime treat!

8-oz. pkg. cream cheese,
  softened
1/2 c. mayonnaise
5 strips bacon, fried and
  crumbled

1 T. green onion, chopped
1/2 t. dill weed
1/8 t. pepper
1 pkg. frozen mini bagels
8 oz. pecans, chopped

Combine first six ingredients, mixing until creamy. Spread on toasted mini-bagels. Sprinkle on chopped pecans and refrigerate until serving time.

An old bean pot becomes a perfect gift when filled with assorted dried beans and favorite recipes.

Sourdough Starter

*Carol Bull
Gooseberry Patch*

Share your starter with a friend!

1/4 c. milk
3/4 c. water
2 t. salad oil
2 t. sugar

1-1/2 t. salt
1 pkg. yeast
2-1/3 c. flour

Combine milk, 1/2 cup water and oil and bring to a boil. Cool to luke-warm and add sugar and salt. Dissolve yeast in 1/4 cup warm water. Add to cooled milk. Stir in flour, blending thoroughly. Cover and let stand in a warm place for 12 to 18 hours to sour. This is enough starter for 12 loaves of bread. It may be divided up and frozen. Bring to room temperature before baking. Maximum storage time for starter is one week in the refrigerator or one month in the freezer.

According to popular folklore, sourdough starter traveled by covered wagon with the American pioneers as they moved westward. It only took a small amount of starter to create generations of delicious sourdough bread!

Sourdough French Bread

Carol Bull
Gooseberry Patch

Makes great sandwiches!

1 pkg. dry yeast
1/4 c. warm water
4-1/2 t. sugar
2-1/2 t. salt
1 c. water

1-1/2 T. solid shortening
1/2 c. milk
2 T. starter dough
4-1/2 c. flour

Dissolve yeast in water in a large bowl, adding sugar and salt. Let rest while bringing one cup of water, shortening and milk to boil in a pan. Cool to lukewarm and pour into yeast mixture, stirring well. Pour slowly over flour; mix all thoroughly. Add starter dough and stir, do not knead. Place dough in greased bowl, cover and let stand until doubled in size. Turn onto a board sprinkled with flour to prevent sticking. Cut dough in half with sharp knife and flatten each half, roll into tapered loaves. Place on a greased cookie sheet, make 1/4-inch slits in the top of each loaf and let rise, uncovered, until doubled in size. Bake 15 minutes at 450 degrees; bake 15 to 20 minutes longer at 350 degrees. Brush with milk and bake 5 minutes longer.

Surprise someone at mealtime with a warm loaf of bread and a crock of whipped butter!

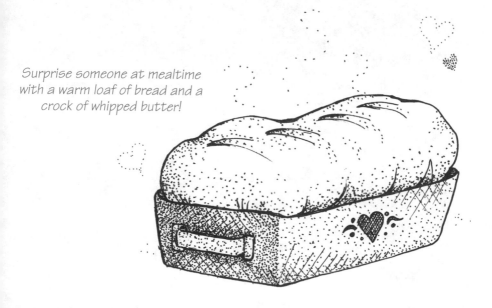

Potato Soup

Ruth Ann Geiger
Marysville, OH

Try Yukon Gold potatoes for a special flavor.

8 slices bacon, fried and
    crumbled
1 c. onion, chopped
2 c. potatoes, chopped
1 c. water
10-3/4 oz. can cream of chicken
    soup

1 c. sour cream
1-3/4 c. milk
1 T. parsley, chopped
1/2 t. salt
dash of pepper

Fry bacon and crumble. Set aside, reserving some drippings in skillet. Sauté onion in same skillet until transparent. Add potatoes to water and boil until tender, about 15 minutes. Add soup, sour cream, milk, bacon and onions, parsley, salt and pepper. Mix well and let simmer 2 hours.

Let your child wrap gifts this year. So what if they're not exactly the way you would have wrapped them...Grandma will be delighted anyway!

Zesty Vegetable Soup

Cyndie Noethen
Montpelier, OH

Great served with hot bread sticks and tossed salad.

1 lb. ground round
1 medium onion, chopped
2 13-3/4 oz. cans beef broth
2 14-1/2 oz. cans Italian
   tomatoes

1 t. Italian seasoning
salt and pepper to taste
1-lb. bag frozen mixed
   vegetables
1/2 c. elbow macaroni

Brown ground round and onion in a medium stock pot. Drain excess fat and add beef broth, tomatoes, and seasonings. Simmer for 20 minutes. Add frozen vegetables and elbow macaroni and continue to simmer over low heat for 30 to 40 minutes.

Bring your favorite childhood Teddy bear down from the attic. Place him under the Christmas tree...sure to rekindle fond memories!

Elf Muffins

Delores E. Hollenbeck
Omaha, NE

I make Elf Muffins as part of a Scandinavian custom. An almond is placed in one muffin and it's believed that whoever eats that muffin will have a year of good health, happiness and fortune. One year we had a large family gathering on both Christmas Eve and Christmas, so I made a larger-than-usual batch of muffins; however I only placed one almond in the entire batch. After our young nephew, Bill, had eaten several muffins and still couldn't find the "lucky elf muffin," I had to tell him Grandma Noble had found it the day before!

Muffins:

1-1/2 c. flour
2 t. baking powder
1/2 t. salt
1/2 t. nutmeg
1/2 c. sugar
1/3 c. shortening

1 egg
1/3 c. milk
1 t. vanilla flavoring
1 t. almond flavoring
1-1/2 c. apples, peeled and
   shredded

Topping:

1 c. butter, melted
3/4 c. sugar

1-1/2 t. cinnamon
1 almond

Sift together first four muffin ingredients and set aside. Cream sugar and shortening; add egg and milk, stirring well. Combine these with the dry ingredients. Add vanilla and almond flavoring, then stir in apples. Fill small, well-greased muffin pans two-thirds full with batter. Insert the almond into any muffin cup. Bake muffins at 400 degrees for 15 to 20 minutes or until golden in color. Remove from pan and cool briefly, then dip into the topping mixture. Makes 36 small muffins.

Cover your pomanders with a rectangle of netting and close at the top with ribbons. Hang on your tree with a satin ribbon loop.

Ham & Cheese Chowder

Tom Huston
Oil City, PA

Great on a cold night with crusty bread, a glass of wine and friends!

3 c. water
4 medium potatoes, pared and diced
1 c. celery, chopped
1 c. carrots, pared and sliced
1-1/4 c. onions, diced
2 t. salt
1/4 t. pepper

1/2 c. butter or margarine
1/2 c. flour
1 qt. milk
4 c. sharp Cheddar cheese, cubed or shredded
2 c. ham, cooked and cubed
pepper sauce to taste (optional)

Add potatoes, celery, carrots, onion, salt and pepper to boiling water. Cover and simmer 10 minutes or until tender. Melt butter in large saucepan or pot; blend in flour. Gradually stir in milk and cook over medium heat until mixture boils. Stir constantly! Add cheese and stir until melted. Add undrained vegetables and ham, heating thoroughly (but not to boiling), then add pepper sauce.

Make-Ahead Dinner Rolls

Clara Hilton
Marengo, OH

A County Fair Blue Ribbon Winner...so easy for busy days!

1 cake compressed or pkg. dry
   yeast
1/2 c. sugar
1 c. warm milk (not hot)

2 eggs, beaten
1/2 c. butter, melted
1 t. salt
4 c. flour

Mix together first three ingredients and let stand for 30 minutes. Add next three ingredients, then mix in flour, two cups at a time. Let stand at room temperature overnight. The next morning, divide the dough in half, rolling each into a 9-inch circle. Cut each circle into twelve equal pie-shaped wedges (a pizza cutter works great!) and roll up beginning at the wide end. Place on a well-greased cookie sheet and let stand until ready to bake. Rolls can stand for 8 to 12 hours, but for best results don't exceed 6 hours. Bake at 375 degrees for 12 to 15 minutes.

Wide, bright rolls of organdy ribbons can be used all around the house...as curtain tiebacks, to dress up lampshades and flowerpots, around your tree as a stunning garland!

Mom's Manhattan Clam Chowder

Patricia Damers
Smithtown, NY

Simple to make...really hits the spot on a cold winter's day! My mom first made this soup when I was a youngster. Now I'm making it for my family!

3 slices bacon
1/2 c. onion, chopped
1/2 c. celery, chopped
1 c. potatoes, diced
1 carrot, shredded
1-1/2 c. water

1 t. salt
8-oz. can minced clams with
   juice
1/4 t. thyme
8-oz. can tomato sauce

Cut the bacon into 1/2-inch pieces and brown in a heavy 3-quart kettle or saucepan until crisp. Add onion and celery to bacon and drippings; sauté until onion is tender. Add potatoes, carrot, water and salt. Cover and simmer 20 minutes. Add clams and clam juice, thyme and tomato sauce. Bring to a simmer just long enough to heat through. Makes 4, one-cup servings.

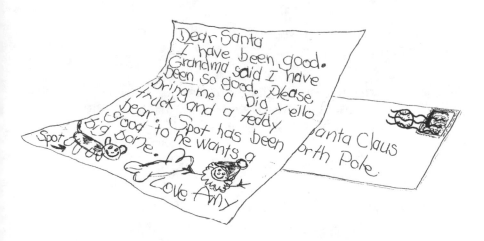

Have your child make some paper snowflakes for Grandma and Grandpa (or far-away relatives) this year. They're so easy to mail, and a treat to receive. They're also great to mail to our servicemen and women spending the holidays away from home. (Check with your local government office for a listing of addresses.)

Colonial Brown Bread

Kathy Bolyea
Naples, FL

Served with prime rib, it's a family tradition!

2 c. whole wheat flour
1/2 c. plus 3 T. flour
1 c. brown sugar, packed

2 t. baking soda
2 c. buttermilk

Mix all dry ingredients, then slowly add buttermilk until well blended.
Pour into a greased loaf pan and bake at 350 degrees for one hour.

Easy Cheese Bread

Kathy Bolyea
Naples, FL

A great accompaniment to your favorite soup or chowder.

2-1/2 c. biscuit mix
1 c. shredded cheese, any type
2 t. poppy seeds

1 egg
1 c. milk

Combine first three ingredients, then combine egg and milk, gradually
add to biscuit mix. Stir vigorously for one minute. Spoon into a greased
loaf pan and bake at 350 degrees for 35 minutes.

*Turn old spools into candleholders! Place spools of different sizes in the
center of your table and surround with greenery, holly and pinecones.*

Empire State Muffins

Dorothy J. Carlson
Allegany, NY

These make a meal in themselves and are so delicious!

1-1/3 c. sugar
2 c. apples, unpeeled and
    shredded
1 c. cranberries, chopped
1 c. carrots, shredded
1 c. walnuts or pecans, chopped
2-1/2 c. all-purpose flour

1 T. baking powder
2 t. baking soda
1/2 t. salt
2 t. cinnamon
2 eggs, slightly beaten
1/2 c. vegetable oil

In a large bowl, combine sugar and apples. Gently fold in cranberries, carrots and nuts. Combine dry ingredients; add to mixing bowl and blend well to moisten. Combine eggs and oil, stir into apple mixture. Grease 18 2-1/2 inch muffin tins and fill two-thirds full. Bake in a 375 degree oven for 20 to 23 minutes; cool 5 minutes before removing from tins. You can also use 4-inch muffin tins and bake about 5 minutes longer.

Snowflake-shaped sugar cookies
with white icing and glittery
sugar are magical!

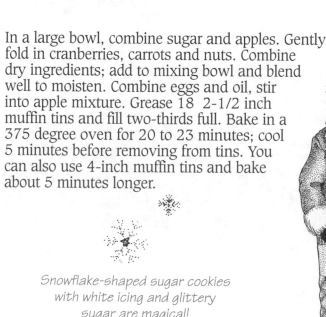

Italian Sausage Soup

Shirll Kosmal
Gooseberry Patch

This recipe is a favorite! It's traveled across Ohio to Pennsylvania,
Florida and California!

2 lbs. mild or hot Italian sausage
2 cloves garlic, minced
2 large onions, chopped
28 oz. whole tomatoes
6 14-oz. cans beef broth
1-1/2 c. red wine, optional
1/2 t. basil

1/2 t. salt
1-1/2 t. Worcestershire sauce
2 t. hot pepper sauce
3 T. parsley
1 medium green pepper, chopped
2 medium zucchini, sliced
3 c. pasta shells, cooked

In a large pot, cook sausage for about 15 minutes. Pierce with fork to release fat and drain. Cut into bite-sized pieces. Add all ingredients except zucchini and pasta. Cook for 30 to 45 minutes, then add zucchini and cook until tender. Add pasta shells just to heat through.

Team up an old cast-iron skillet and some stone-ground cornmeal for a cook on your Christmas list.

Savory Herb Biscuits

Jackie Hoover
Newark, OH

Delicious and very easy!

2 c. biscuit mix
1/2 c. Cheddar cheese, shredded
2/3 c. milk
1/4 c. butter or margarine,
    melted

1/2 t. garlic powder
1/2 t. basil, dried

Preheat oven to 450 degrees. Combine biscuit mix, cheese and milk until a soft dough forms. Beat vigorously for 30 seconds. Drop by heaping tablespoonfuls onto an ungreased cookie sheet. Bake for 10 to 12 minutes, or until golden brown. Combine basil and garlic powder with melted butter and brush over hot biscuits after removing from oven. Makes 12 biscuits.

Begin stocking your pantry in the fall with those things you'll be needing for baking around the holidays...chocolate chips, vanilla, dried and candied fruits, sugar and flour.

Pumpkin Bread

Kimberly Burns
Gooseberry Patch

A slice of this bread with a hot cup of tea will hit the spot!

16-oz. can pumpkin
3 c. sugar
1 c. oil
2/3 c. water
4 eggs
3-1/2 c. flour

2 t. soda
1-1/2 t. salt
1 t. cinnamon
1 t. nutmeg
1/2 t. ginger

Preheat oven to 350 degrees. Grease the bottoms and sides of two 9"x5" or 8"x4" loaf pans; set aside. In a large bowl blend first five ingredients at medium speed for one minute. Add remaining ingredients and blend at low speed until moistened, then beat one minute at medium speed. Pour batter into prepared pans and bake at 350 degrees for 60 to 75 minutes, or until a toothpick inserted in the center comes out clean. Cool 5 minutes, then remove from pans and cool completely. Serve with cream cheese spread.

Cream Cheese Spread

8 oz. light cream cheese
1/4 c. light margarine

3/4 or 1 c. powdered sugar

Beat cream cheese and margarine together at medium speed. Add powdered sugar slowly, beating until smooth. Serve with pumpkin bread!

Banana Muffins

Judy Young
Plano, TX

Top these muffins with cinnamon sugar, almonds or chocolate chips for a different flavor!

3 large ripe bananas	1-1/2 c. all-purpose flour
3/4 c. sugar	1/2 t. salt, optional
1 egg, slightly beaten	1 t. baking soda
1/3 c. butter or margarine, melted	1 t. baking powder

Mash bananas, then add sugar, egg and butter. Combine with dry ingredients, mixing well. Pour into a muffin pan and bake at 375 degrees for 20 minutes.

Make your own mini tree! Place evergreen boughs of different sizes in an old crock, placing the tallest ones in the middle. Decorate with tiny beeswax ornaments or ribbons of homespun.

MEMORABLE
Main Dishes

Pork Crown Roast with Fruit Glaze

Cathy Moore
Powell, OH

The crowning glory of your Christmas groaning board.

1-1/2 t. fennel seed, crushed
1-1/2 t. onion powder
1 t. salt

1 t. pepper
8 lb. pork crown roast
vegetable oil

Combine all ingredients in a small bowl, except for the roast and oil. Rub this mixture on all sides of the roast, cover and refrigerate overnight. Brush the roast lightly with vegetable oil and insert a meat thermometer. Cover the bone ends with foil and place roast on a rack in a 325 degree oven. Roast until a meat thermometer reads 165 degrees. Allow to stand for 10 minutes before carving. Makes 8 to 10 servings.

Fruit Glaze:

1/2 c. dried apricot halves
1/2 c. dried peach halves
3/4 c. apple juice, divided
1/4 t. ground cardamom

2 t. cornstarch
1 c. seedless green grapes
1 c. seedless red grapes

In a 1-1/2 quart casserole, combine fruit, 1/2 cup of apple juice and cardamom. Cover casserole dish and microwave on high power for 6 minutes, or until fruit begins to fill out. In a separate bowl, combine corn starch and remaining apple juice, stirring well. Add to fruit mixture and microwave on high power for 2 minutes, or until thick. Add grapes, stir gently and spoon as a garnish around pork roast.

Roast Vermont Turkey

Jo Ann

A classic New England dish served with sausage stuffing!

20 lb. turkey   1 onion, peeled and quartered
salt and pepper

Remove giblets from the turkey and thoroughly rinse cavity. Pat dry and sprinkle salt and pepper inside the cavity. Place turkey in a preheated 325 degree oven, breast side up, in a roasting pan. Insert a meat thermometer in the thigh and cover legs with foil. Roast for 1-1/2 hours, basting often. Remove the foil and roast for an additional 1-1/2 hours or until a meat thermometer registers 180 degrees. Allow turkey to rest 20 minutes before carving.

Don't forget to check the batteries in your camera! Stock up on extra batteries for toys, film, light bulbs and hooks for your ornaments.

Sausage Stuffing

Carol Sheets
Gooseberry Patch

A great recipe from one of the best cooks we know!

1/4 c. butter
5 c. French bread, cubed
1/2 lb. pork sausage
1 small onion, chopped
1/3 c. celery, thinly sliced

1 medium apple, cored and
   chopped
1/2 c. pecans or walnuts,
   chopped
1/3 c. chicken broth

Melt butter over medium heat in a large skillet. Add bread cubes, stirring well to coat. Over medium heat, continue to cook crumbs until bread is lightly toasted. Place in a mixing bowl and set aside. Using the same skillet, cook sausage over medium heat, breaking up and stirring until completely done. Add onion and celery, cooking until tender. Remove from heat and add to bread crumb mixture. Add apples and nuts, mixing thoroughly. Add broth. In a greased 1-1/2 quart casserole dish, bake dressing covered for 30 minutes at 350 degrees. Remove cover from casserole and bake an additional 15 to 25 minutes until thoroughly heated.

Need a little glow for your holiday dinner party? If you don't have a dimmer on your dining room light switch, try replacing the light bulbs in your light fixture with a lower wattage pink or golden yellow bulb. Add a few sparkling candles on the table for a warm glow that fills the room.

Garlic-Dijon Puff Pastry Ham

Vickie

Pre-made puff pastry makes it so easy, and your guests will love it!

2 boxes frozen puff pastry
3/4 lb. smoked ham
3 eggs
2 t. garlic

oil
1-1/2 c. mayonnaise
1/4 c. Dijon mustard

Preheat oven to 400 degrees. Thaw puff pastry well. Wrap ham with dough, sealing entire ham inside of dough. Using mini cutters, cut out shapes from remaining dough and decorate ham. Brush well with egg and and bake in oven for approximately 45 minutes. When puff pastry is brown, cover with aluminum foil. Sauté garlic in small amount of oil, being careful not to burn. Add mayonnaise, mixing well. After one minute, add mustard and heat slowly for 2 more minutes. Serve garlic mayonnaise in a side dish.

Fill crockery bowls with oranges and lemons studded with cloves. Bright, festive and fragrant!

Scallop Casserole

Marcia Dearnley
Connellsville, PA

Try this recipe with a mixture of shrimp and scallops.

1 lb. scallops, fresh or thawed
1/4 c. white wine
1/2 lb. butter, melted

1/2 sleeve round butter crackers, crushed
salt and pepper to taste
dash of lemon

Marinate scallops in wine for 10 minutes, then rinse in colander and pat dry. Stir with melted butter and cracker crumbs. Place in a one-quart casserole dish, add salt, pepper and lemon. Bake at 350 degrees uncovered for 20 minutes, turning halfway through cooking time. Serves 2 as a main dish, 4 as a side dish.

To give your holiday garland a homespun touch, string tiny rag balls and old spools along with your apple and orange slices.

Roast Chicken Dinner

Lee Shears
Delaware, OH

Remove skin from chicken pieces for a healthy, hearty dish.

2 10-3/4 oz. cans cream of
    chicken soup
1-1/2 cans water

3/4 c. rice
3 or 4 lb. chicken, whole or
    cut-up fryer or roaster

Mix soup, water and rice and pour in a roaster or casserole dish. Place chicken on top of soup mixture, then sprinkle with salt and pepper. Cover and bake at 350 degrees for 3 hours. Remove cover during last half hour to allow chicken to brown.

Roast Beef

Kathy Williamson
Gooseberry Patch

Makes a delicious gravy.

4 or 5 lb. rump roast
8-oz. bottle Italian dressing

4 t. soy sauce
garlic powder to taste

Place beef in a casserole dish or Dutch oven and cover with Italian dressing. Add soy sauce, cover and let marinate overnight. Before placing in oven, lightly season with garlic powder. Cover and bake at 375 degrees for 2-1/2 hours.

Yorkshire Pudding

Nancy Dandeneau
Troy, NY

This recipe was one of my mother's favorites. It was passed down to my mother from her mother who came from England.

1 c. flour
1/2 t. baking powder
1/2 t. salt
1 c. milk

2 egg yolks
1 T. shortening, melted
2 egg whites

Mix and sift flour, baking powder and salt. Add milk, beaten egg yolks and shortening, mixing well, gently fold in egg whites. Cover the bottom of a 10-inch baking dish with drippings from the roast beef. Pour batter into baking dish and bake in a hot oven at 400 degrees for 20 minutes. After the pudding has risen, baste with drippings from the roast. When done, cut into squares or wedges and serve on a platter with roast beef.

Give a gardener friend a nicely braided string of garlic, or share some bulbs from your garden.

Glazed Cornish Game Hens

Liz Kenneweg
Gooseberry Patch

Hens are just right for a candlelight dinner for two.

1/4 c. red current jelly
pinch of cinnamon
2 Cornish game hens

1/4 t. salt
pepper

Combine jelly and cinnamon, mixing well. Microwave on high power until jelly melts; set aside. Remove giblets from hens; then rinse and pat dry. Sprinkle cavities with salt and pepper and secure legs with string. Place hens in a roasting pan, cover loosely with foil and bake in a 350 degree oven for one hour. Brush hens with current glaze, return to oven and roast for an additional 30 minutes or until golden.

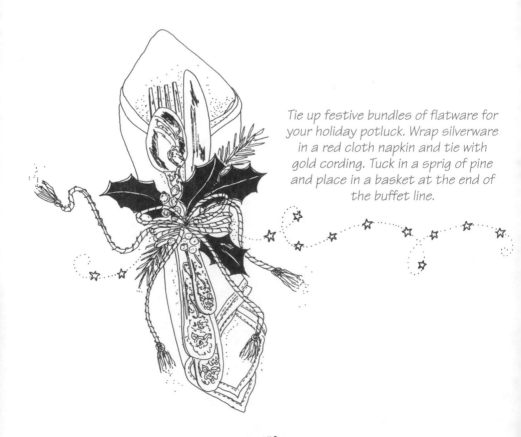

Tie up festive bundles of flatware for your holiday potluck. Wrap silverware in a red cloth napkin and tie with gold cording. Tuck in a sprig of pine and place in a basket at the end of the buffet line.

Creamy Mushroom & Ham Ravioli

Sally McArthur
Ostrander, OH

Ready-made ravioli makes this recipe a snap!

9-oz. pkg. refrigerated cheese
　ravioli or tortellini
2 T. butter
1/4 c. red bell pepper, chopped
4.5-oz. jar sliced mushrooms,
　drained
1/2 c. water

3/4 c. milk
4 t. cornstarch
1 t. chicken-flavored instant
　bouillon
1 c. ham, cubed
3/4 c. frozen peas

Cook ravioli as directed on package, then drain. Melt butter in large skillet over medium heat. Add peppers and mushrooms; sauté. In small bowl combine water, milk, cornstarch and bouillon, blending well. Add to skillet and cook until mixture thickens and boils, stirring constantly. Stir in ham, peas and ravioli, heat thoroughly. Makes 4 1-1/2 cup servings.

Fill baskets with pine-cones and other natural delights found in fields or nearby woods.

Creamy Chicken Enchiladas

LaRayne Cummons
Lakeview, OH

Only 20 minutes to prepare!

2 c. chicken, cooked and
  shredded
1 c. green peppers, diced
16 oz. picante sauce
8 oz. cream cheese

10-count pkg. flour tortillas
1 lb. spicy pasteurized processed
  cheese spread
1/4 c. milk
2 cans black olives, sliced

Stir chicken, green peppers, one cup picante sauce and cream cheese in skillet over low heat until smooth. Spoon 1/4 cup chicken mixture onto each tortilla, roll up and place seam-side down in a 12"x9" pan. In same skillet heat the processed cheese with milk over low heat. Stir until melted and smooth. Pour sauce over tortillas. Sprinkle black olives over top and spoon remaining picante sauce over this. Cover with foil and bake 25 minutes, or until thoroughly heated. Serve with salsa and sour cream on the side.

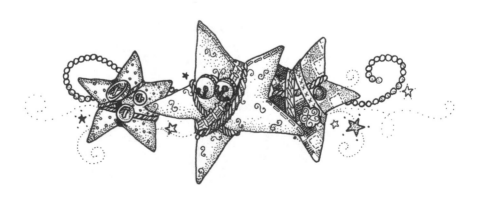

Decorate tiny gingerbread hearts with stripes and dots for your feather tree.

Lemon Deluxe Chicken

Wendy Lee Paffenroth
Pine Island, NY

A bit different and tasty...never any leftovers!

1/2 c. lemon juice
1 t. garlic powder
8-oz. bottle Italian salad dressing
1 pkg. chicken bouillion

6 oz. water
1 onion, sliced thin and
   separated
8 chicken breasts, skinned

Combine all the sauce ingredients and pour in a casserole dish over the chicken. Place covered chicken in the refrigerator for at least 4 hours or overnight. Place in an ovenproof baking dish and bake for about 45 minutes in a 350 degree oven. Five minutes before serving, put under the broiler to brown the chicken. Watch so it doesn't burn! Makes 5 to 6 servings. Serve with rice and a vegetable or salad.

Tiny mittens or toddler socks look wonderful framed as a gift to grandparents, or to the child they belonged to once upon a time.

Lori's Cabin Chicken

Desi Rader
Delaware, OH

Every year I go on vacation with my sisters, mom and aunt. We stay in a beautiful cabin on an island in Canada on a seven-mile lake. The one-room cabin is made of logs and very primitive. We use a generator for lights, propane to cook and an outhouse for, well you know! We pump water from the lake for dishes and heat it on the stove. We love fast, easy recipes, and this one is delicious too!

4 boneless chicken breasts, cut into pieces
1/4 c. Italian salad dressing
2 c. white rice
2 c. Cheddar cheese, shredded
2 large tomatoes, chopped
4 or 6 green onions, chopped
12-oz. jar of chicken gravy, warmed
12-oz. can lo mein noodles

Sauté chicken in salad dressing over high heat for 10 minutes or until thoroughly done. Prepare rice according to package directions. Place each of the remaining ingredients in a separate bowl.

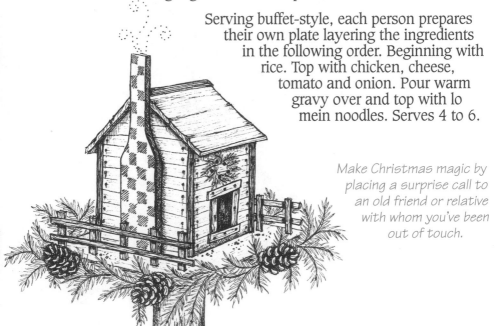

Serving buffet-style, each person prepares their own plate layering the ingredients in the following order. Beginning with rice. Top with chicken, cheese, tomato and onion. Pour warm gravy over and top with lo mein noodles. Serves 4 to 6.

Make Christmas magic by placing a surprise call to an old friend or relative with whom you've been out of touch.

Traditional Christmas Goose

Liz Kenneweg
Gooseberry Patch

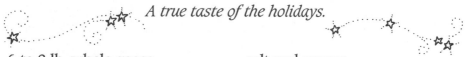

A true taste of the holidays.

6 to 8 lb. whole goose   salt and pepper

Heat oven to 325 degrees. Rinse the goose thoroughly and pat dry. Sprinkle salt and pepper in the cavity, secure legs together with string and tuck wing tips under. Using a large roasting pan, place goose breast side up and sprinkle with salt and pepper. Roast goose for 20 to 25 minutes per pound, basting often. Drain excess fat with a turkey baster during roasting. Legs will move freely and juice will run clear when done. Serves 6 to 8.

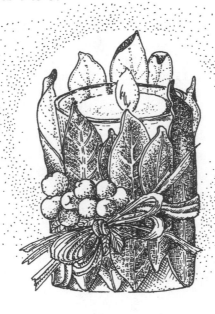

Light an entire room with thick pillar candles set inside hurricane globes. The globes provide an old-fashioned, romantic glow for the room, and keep flames safely covered.

Tourtiere Pork Pie

Joan Brochu
Hardwick, VT

This is a delicious recipe and wonderful to have on hand in your freezer for a busy day. Add a tossed salad and you have a wonderful dinner!

1 lb. lean ground pork
2 lbs. lean ground beef
1 large onion, diced
3 russet potatoes, diced
3/4 t. allspice
3/4 t. cinnamon

3/4 t. cloves
salt and pepper to taste
3/4 t. garlic powder
9" prepared pastry shell or your
    favorite homemade pie crust
    recipe

Put ground meat in a large pan, add onion and potatoes. Barely cover with water and cook until meat is no longer pink. After 15 minutes, add spices. Keep mixture covered with water. After it's completely cooked, cool. When the fat has settled on the top, remove and discard. Add additional salt, pepper and spices according to taste. Place in pie shell and bake at 350 degrees for 1/2 hour.

Make old-fashioned soap stars for a tiny grapevine tree! Using a sharp knife, cut along the length of a bar of pure, white soap making slices 1/4-inch thick. Slowly press a mini cookie cutter into the soap, pop out the stars, and tuck in among the grapevines.

Cranberry-Glazed Pork Roast

Doris Stegner
Gooseberry Patch

Plan to serve pork for the New Year...it's good luck!

4 lb. boneless pork loin roast
2 t. cornstarch
1/4 t. cinnamon
1/8 t. salt

1/2 t. orange peel, grated
2 T. orange juice
16 oz. whole berry cranberry
    sauce

In a small saucepan, stir together all ingredients except pork. Cook, stirring over medium heat until thickened; set aside. Place roast in shallow baking dish. Roast at 325 degrees for 45 minutes. Spoon 1/2-cup glaze over roast and continue roasting for 30 to 45 minutes or until meat thermometer reads 155 to 160 degrees. Let stand 10 minutes before slicing and serve with remaining sauce. Serves 16.

Purchase a bright red tablecloth for Christmas. Each year ask everyone who eats at your holiday table to write their name and the year on the tablecloth. During the winter months, embroider each signature and date with embroidery floss. Bring out the tablecloth again for the next holiday!

Baked Maple Ham

Becky Sykes
Gooseberry Patch

Make sure there's plenty left over for sandwiches and casseroles!

1-1/4 c. dark brown sugar,
   firmly packed
1/3 c. maple syrup

cloves
8 or 10 lb. precooked ham

Preheat oven to 350 degrees. Combine brown sugar and syrup, mixing well. Place ham in a roasting pan and bake for 70 minutes. Remove ham from oven and score top of ham in a diamond pattern using a sharp knife. Insert cloves in the ham and brush brown sugar and syrup mixture over ham. Return ham to oven and bake for an additional 20 minutes.

Keep wrapping materials handy. Put wrapping paper, ribbon, tags, scissors and tape in a large basket next to the fireplace or under an end table. You'll be ready to lend a hand for last-minute wrapping projects.

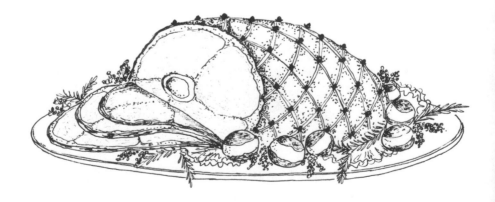

Beef, Pasta & Artichoke Toss

Molly Bordonaro
Worthington, OH

Good balsamic vinegar makes the dish.

1-1/2 lb. boneless beef sirloin
   steak, cut 1-inch thick
4 c. tri-colored rotelle pasta,
   uncooked
14-oz. can quartered artichoke
   hearts, drained

1 large red bell pepper, cut into
   julienne strips
1 c. small pitted ripe olives
2 T. fresh basil, thinly sliced

Place beef steak on rack in broiler pan so
surface of meat is 3 to 4 inches from heat.
Broil steak approximately 16 to 18 minutes
for medium-rare to medium doneness,
turning once. Let stand 10 minutes. Trim fat
from steak, cut crosswise in half and then
lengthwise into thin slices. Cook pasta
according to package directions. Drain; rinse
with cold water. In a large bowl, combine
beef, pasta, artichoke hearts, bell pepper,
olives and basil, mixing lightly. Pour
vinaigrette over beef mixture.

Balsamic Vinaigrette:

1/4 c. olive oil
1/4 c. balsamic vinegar
1-1/2 t. dried basil leaves
3/4 t. salt
1/4 t. pepper

In a small bowl, whisk together ingredients and
pour over beef mixture; toss to coat. Cover and
refrigerate at least 2 hours or overnight. Makes 8,
1-1/2 cup servings.

Chicken Divan

Gay Barnhart
Ashley, OH

2 pkgs. frozen broccoli, cooked
2 c. cooked chicken, sliced
2 10 3/4 oz. cans cream of
   chicken soup
1 c. mayonnaise

1 t. lemon juice
1/2 t. curry powder
1/2 c. Cheddar cheese, grated
1/2 c. soft buttered bread
   crumbs or croutons

Place broccoli and chicken in baking dish. Combine soup, mayonnaise, lemon juice and curry powder. Pour over chicken. Sprinkle cheese and bread crumbs over top and bake at 325 degrees for 30 minutes.

Looking for a unique gift idea? Give all the makings for a great Italian dinner! Fill a stockpot with pasta, sauces, garlic, herbs and wooden spoons.

Curry Chicken Casserole

Paulette Kehm-Yelton
Elizabethton, TN

Very easy to put together during the busy Christmas season! Can be made ahead and refrigerated for up to two days until ready to bake!

6 large chicken breasts, cooked
   and chopped
2 10-oz. pkgs. frozen broccoli,
   chopped
2 10-3/4 oz. cans cream of
   chicken soup
1 c. mayonnaise

3/4 or 1 t. curry powder
3 T. lemon juice
8 oz. Cheddar cheese, grated
bread crumbs
2 2-1/2 oz. jars mushrooms,
   sliced

Mix first six ingredients until thoroughly blended and place in a greased 13"x9" pan. Sprinkle cheese, mushrooms and bread crumbs over top. Bake in pre-heated 350 degree oven for 45 minutes. Serves approximately 12.

Various sizes of candlesticks grouped together make a quick, simple mantel arrangement.

Seasonal SALADS and SIDES

Cranberry Waldorf Salad

Judy Carter
Dunnellon, FL

A family tradition.

2 c. raw cranberries
3 c. marshmallows
3/4 c. sugar
1/2 c. walnuts

1/2 c. seedless green grapes
2 c. apples, unpeeled & diced
1 c. whipped cream

Place cranberries in a food processor or blender and chop lightly. Combine cranberries, marshmallows and sugar; chill overnight. Fold in remaining ingredients and serve chilled.

Popcorn that's a little stale will hold together better when you string it for your garland, so pop the popcorn a couple days ahead of time.

Sesame Seafood Salad   *Vickie*

My family loves this one!

1 T. sugar
1 T. cornstarch
1/2 t. salt
1 c. rice vinegar
2 T. water
2 large cucumbers, unpeeled &
    thinly sliced

1 c. celery, sliced
1/4 lb. small shrimp, cooked
1/4 lb. small scallops, cooked
1 T. sesame seeds, toasted

Combine sugar, cornstarch and salt in a saucepan. Add vinegar and water and continue to cook over medium heat until mixture comes to a boil and thickens. Allow to cool, add cucumbers, celery, shrimp, scallops and sesame seeds. Refrigerate at least 2 hours or overnight. Stir well prior to serving.

Seashells collected in the summer make beautiful ornaments in the winter.

Taffy Apple Salad

Mary Murray
Gooseberry Patch

Cool and refreshing!

1 T. flour
1/4 c. sugar
1 egg, slightly beaten
2 T. apple cider vinegar
16-oz. can pineapple tidbits,
    reserve juice

4 c. apples, chopped with skins
8 oz. whipped topping, thawed
2 c. miniature marshmallows
1/2 c. peanuts

Mix flour, sugar, egg, vinegar, and pineapple juice in a saucepan. Simmer until thickened; cool. Stir together pineapple tidbits, apples, whipped topping, marshmallows and 1/4 cup peanuts, combining thoroughly with sauce. Place in a serving bowl and garnish with remaining peanuts.

Fill a basket for the tea lover on your list with a bright red teapot, tea blends, honey dipper and biscuits to snack on!

Frosty Cranberry Mold

Sharon Hall
Gooseberry Patch

A colorful addition to your holiday table.

1 lb. 4-oz. can crushed
   pineapple
1-lb. can whole cranberry sauce
2 3-oz. pkgs. raspberry gelatin,
   regular or sugar-free
8-oz. pkg. cream cheese,
   softened

2 T. salad dressing
1 c. heavy cream or 9-oz. pkg.
   whipped topping
1/2 c. walnuts, coarsely chopped
1 tart apple, peeled and chopped
1/2 c. celery, chopped

Drain fruit, reserving liquid. Pour gelatin in medium bowl, add one cup water and stir until gelatin is thoroughly dissolved. Add water to reserved juice until mixture equals one cup. Stir into dissolved gelatin mixture and chill until partially set. Beat softened cream cheese and salad dressing together until fluffy. Gradually beat in chilled gelatin, then fold this mixture into whipped cream or topping. Set aside 1-1/2 cups of this mixture for frosting. Add drained fruit, nuts, apple and celery to remaining mixture and pour into two 8-inch glass dishes. Refrigerate until surface is set, about 20 minutes. Frost with the reserved mixture and refrigerate for several hours.

Gather a large bouquet of eucalyptus with a wide tartan bow and place in an old washstand.

Winter Salad

Barbara Bargdill
Gooseberry Patch

A hearty salad, full of vitamins!

1 bunch broccoli, cut in small
   pieces
1 head cauliflower, cut in small
   pieces
1 medium red onion, sliced thin,
   separated in rings

1/2 lb. fresh mushrooms, sliced
1/4 c. raisins, optional
1/2 lb. bacon, fried and
   crumbled
1/4 c. slivered almonds, toasted

Dressing:

1-1/2 c. mayonnaise
1/3 c. sugar

3 T. vinegar

Gently mix all salad ingredients. Blend dressing ingredients thoroughly.
Fold dressing into vegetable mixture and refrigerate at least 1 to 2
hours before serving. Sprinkle with almonds. Makes 8 to 10 servings.

*Add warm candlelight to your home. Place a fat candle in a canning jar, remove
the lid and replace the ring.*

Fruit Salad with Orange Dressing

Shirll Kosmal
Gooseberry Patch

Add any fruits in season to this special dressing.

2 6.1-oz. cans mandarin
   oranges, drained
2 15-oz. cans sliced peaches,
   drained
2 1 lb. 4-oz. cans pineapple
   tidbits, drained
1 apple with skin, diced

3/4 c. sour cream
3-oz. box instant vanilla
   pudding
1-1/2 c. milk
6-oz. container frozen orange
   juice concentrate (do not add
   water)

Mix all fruits together in a large bowl. Whisk together pudding mix and milk; stir in orange juice until melted. Pour over fruit and refrigerate overnight.

bountiful

blessings

Fill wooden bowls, crocks and dishes throughout your holiday home with French lavender buds, rose hips, dried orange slices, star anise, dried pomegranates and cinnamon sticks.

Chicken & Shrimp Salad

Henrietta Strunk
Oakland, TX

A festive, hearty salad for special occasions.

1 fryer chicken, boiled, deboned
    and cut in bite-sized pieces
4 medium potatoes, peeled,
    boiled, and diced

2 lbs. shrimp, boiled and peeled
1 can water chestnuts, drained

Combine all ingredients and coat with sauce.

Sauce:

2 c. mayonnaise
8 oz. cream cheese, softened
1 or 2 green onions, finely
    chopped
2 T. Dijon mustard

1/2 c. lemon juice
2 T. parsley, chopped
2 T. capers, chopped
salt and pepper to taste

Whisk all ingredients together until well blended.

The perfect container for kitchen gifts: a crock the cook will love! Fill with a rolling pin and wooden spoons.

Oyster Stuffing

Mable Covey
Sheridan, MI

Oysters add an indescribably rich flavor.

1 large sweet onion, chopped
1/2 lb. butter
1 c. celery, chopped
2 T. parsley
1 T. salt
1 t. pepper
1 T. garlic salt
1/2 t. thyme

2 T. ground sage
1 t. poultry seasoning
2 large loaves white bread, torn
2 large eggs, beaten
1 pt. oysters and liquid
1/2 t. onion salt
2 c. milk

Mix all of the above ingredients together, blending well. Stuff turkey cavities loosely, (stuffing will swell as it's baked), then place the turkey in a large roasting pan and bake at 350 degrees for 4 to 5 hours, or until done. Can also be baked in a casserole dish at 350 degrees for one hour as a side dish.

Barley Casserole

Jackie Hoover
Newark, OH

A warm cozy wintertime dish.

1/2 c. onion, finely chopped
5 T. butter, divided
1/2 c. barley

3 c. chicken broth
1-1/2 c. fresh mushrooms, sliced

Sauté onion in 3 tablespoons butter, add barley and brown. Put in a 1-1/2 quart casserole dish with 1-1/2 cups chicken broth. Cover and bake at 350 degrees for 30 minutes. Sauté mushrooms in remaining butter. After 30 minutes, add mushrooms with remaining chicken broth. Bake covered for one hour longer. If there is a lot of liquid remaining, remove cover and bake 5 minutes longer. Casserole should be moist, but not liquid.

Spinach Casserole

Cindy B. D'Angelo
Bordentown, NJ

One of our family's favorite recipes.

4 10-oz. pkgs. spinach, chopped
1 pt. sour cream
1 pkg. onion soup mix

2 c. crumb-style herb stuffing
3/4 stick of butter

Cook spinach according to package directions; drain well. Mix with sour cream and soup mix. Put mixture in 13"x9"x2" casserole. Cover top with stuffing. Melt butter and pour over stuffing; bake 15 minutes at 350 degrees. Serves 20.

soft candles glow

Asparagus Casserole

Donna Magraw
Canandaigua, NY

This recipe was given to me many years ago by my aunt. It's a favorite side dish!

2 T. butter, melted
12 spears fresh asparagus, or
   10-oz. pkg. frozen (not
   canned)
2 T. onion, diced

2 T. Parmesan cheese, grated
1/4 c. bread crumbs
1/2 t. salt
1/8 t. pepper
1/8 t. oregano

Put butter in shallow square baking dish. Line bottom with asparagus spears. Mix remaining ingredients together and spread over spears. Cover and bake 30 to 45 minutes at 375 degrees.

To help gingerbread cookie ornaments retain their shape, omit the baking soda!

Honey-Orange Carrots

Janet Davis
Antioch, CA

Bright and cheerful on your holiday table.

8 or 10 medium carrots, peeled
   and cut into 3-inch sticks
7 t. butter
2 T. sesame seeds

1 T. honey
1 T. orange rind, grated
1 t. fresh ginger, grated

Steam carrots until tender, about 15 minutes. While carrots steam, melt one teaspoon butter in medium fry pan and toast sesame seeds until golden. When carrots are tender, add remaining butter, honey, orange rind and ginger to the pan. Remove carrots from the steamer and add to the pan. Toss to coat.

Mashed Potato Soufflé

Deborah L. Crosby
Cinnaminson, NJ

Dress up your mashed potatoes for Christmas.

10 or 12 potatoes, boiled,
   mashed and seasoned with
   salt, pepper and milk
3 T. Parmesan cheese
4 eggs, beaten

2 t. onion, chopped
16-oz. pkg. mozzarella cheese,
   grated
bread crumbs
parsley

After potatoes are cooked and mashed, add Parmesan cheese, eggs and onion. Spray a 13"x9"x3" casserole with non-stick cooking spray, then layer potatoes and mozzarella cheese in pan. Top with buttered bread crumbs and parsley. Bake at 375 for 45 to 50 minutes.

Chestnut Stuffing

Vickie

Stuff your turkey with a traditional recipe of New England.

1 lb. whole chestnuts
1 medium onion, chopped
1 T. butter
2 large apples, cored and
   chopped

3/4 c. fresh bread, cubed
1 T. fresh parsley
1/2 t. dried thyme
1/4 t. pepper
1/4 c. chicken stock

Make a cross cut in the flat side of each chestnut using a knife point. Boil chestnuts in 2 quarts of water for 15 to 25 minutes. Drain and cool. Peel chestnuts and cut into quarters. Set aside. In a skillet, combine onion and butter and sauté until tender. Add chestnuts and remaining ingredients, mixing well. Preheat oven to 350 degrees and place stuffing in a greased 1-1/2 quart casserole. Bake dressing covered for 30 minutes. Uncover and bake an additional 15 to 25 minutes.

Place three or four poinsettias in an unused fireplace, string garland on the mantel, hang the stockings and you have a beautiful family photo setting!

Sweet Potato Casserole

Liz Plotnick
Gooseberry Patch

We had this at our Christmas potluck, and it was yummy!

2-1/2 cans (40 oz. each) sweetened yams, drained
16 oz. cranberry sauce, jelled

2 15.25-oz. cans chunk
   pineapple, drained
10.5 oz. mini marshmallows

With an electric mixer, food processor, or fork, mix yams until they
resemble lumpy mashed potatoes. Layer ingredients in baking casserole dish in the following order: yams, pineapple, thin slices of
cranberry sauce and marshmallows. Repeat for second layer, omitting
marshmallows. Bake at 350 degrees until hot in center, add remaining
marshmallows. Once they begin to melt, broil until golden brown.

*Create spongeware sugar cookies! Frost cookies with white royal icing, then
sponge on food colored icing in red, blue, or black. Tie with a big bow and
hang on your tree!*

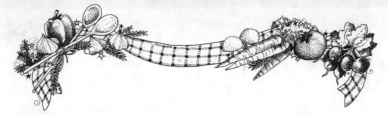

Holiday Spiced Peaches

Carol Volz-Begley
Beaver, PA

Glaze your ham with the wonderful leftover sauce!

3-1/2 c. peach halves, canned
1 T. mixed pickling spices
3 6-inch cinnamon sticks

1 t. whole cloves
1 T. vinegar

In a saucepan combine all ingredients and simmer 5 minutes. Serve warm if placed on a platter with ham; or serve warm or chilled in a bowl as a side dish. Drain before serving. Stud peaches with additional whole cloves if desired. Serves 6.

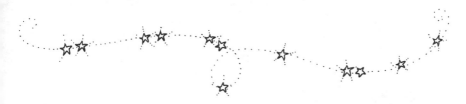

Savannah Red Rice

Esther T. Lee
Carlisle, PA

A delicious side dish with baked ham.

1 lb. bacon
1/2 c. onions, chopped
1/2 c. celery, chopped
4 c. stewed tomatoes

2 c. raw rice
1/2 t. salt
1/4 t. pepper
1/8 t. hot pepper sauce

Fry bacon until crisp and remove from pan, reserving bacon drippings. Cook onions and celery in drippings until tender, then add tomatoes, rice and seasonings. Add crumbled bacon last. Cook over low heat in large frying pan for 10 minutes. Pour into large casserole and cover tightly. Bake at 350 degrees for one hour, stirring with fork several times. Serves 8 to 10.

Pam's Cheese Potatoes

Pamela Hill
Valley Station, KY

We don't know anyone who doesn't like 'em!

5 lb. potatoes, sliced
1 medium onion, diced
1 lb. pasteurized processed
    cheese spread
salt and pepper

10 strips bacon, cooked and
    crumbled
1 stick butter or margarine

Layer potatoes, onion and cheese in ungreased 13"x9" baking dish; salt and pepper to taste. Sprinkle bacon pieces on top and add pats of butter. Bake 30 minutes. Serves 10 to 12.

Core several fresh artichokes and allow them to dry
out. Spray them with gold paint and allow to dry. Tuck
a votive candle in each and set on your table or mantel.

Hot Spiced Fruit

Charlotte Wolfe
Ft. Lauderdale, FL

Serve with your Christmas ham.

2 c. canned peach halves
2 c. canned pear halves
2 c. canned pineapple spears
1/2 c. orange marmalade

2 T. butter
1 cinnamon stick
1/8 T. ground nutmeg
1/8 T. ground cloves

Drain fruit, reserving 1-1/2 cups juice. Combine marmalade, butter, spices and reserved syrup. Bring to a boil; cooking 20 to 30 minutes. Remove spices before serving. Serves 8.

Roasted Redskins Dijon

Molly Bordonaro
Worthington, OH

These are so spicy, who needs butter?

4 T. Dijon mustard
2 t. paprika
1 t. chili powder

1 t. ground cumin
1/2 t. ground red pepper
18 baby redskin potatoes

Preheat oven to 400 degrees. Spray a shallow roasting pan with non-stick cooking spray. In a bowl with a tight-fitting lid, mix spices with mustard, add potatoes, put the lid on and shake until potatoes are well coated. Empty potatoes into roasting pan and prick each one with a fork. Bake for about 35 to 40 minutes, until tender.

Look through your local newspaper for special music and caroling programs and candlelight house tours.

Pasta with Red Pepper & Broccoli

*Molly Bordonaro
Worthington, OH*

A quick, healthy dinner when you're stressed for time!

2 15-oz. cans fat-free chicken
   broth
1 t. lemon peel, grated
black pepper to taste
3 c. broccoli flowerets

1 red pepper, oven-roasted for
   10 minutes, cut into strips
6 oz. angel hair pasta, uncooked
1 T. Romano cheese, grated

Combine broth, lemon peel and pepper in a 4-quart saucepan and bring to a boil. Stir in broccoli, red pepper and pasta; return to a boil. Reduce heat and simmer 3 minutes, stirring frequently until pasta is tender. Transfer to pasta bowls and sprinkle with cheese. Serves 4.

Mexican Rice

*Lee Ann Keener
Corona, CA*

Spice it up with hot sauce on these cold, blustery days.

2 c. rice, cooked
10-3/4 oz. can cream of chicken
   soup
8 oz. sour cream

1 small can green chilies,
   chopped or whole
1/2 c. Cheddar cheese, grated

Mix rice, soup and sour cream. Put half of the rice mixture in a baking dish; add half the grated cheese and chilies. Then put remaining mixture on top with remaining cheese and chilies. Bake or microwave until heated through. Serves 8. Can be made ahead and frozen.

Grandma Tilden's Peanut Coleslaw

Liz Kenneweg
Gooseberry Patch

A Vermont family recipe from the 1800's!

2 eggs, beaten
1/2 c. sugar
1/2 c. vinegar
1/2 t. salt

1/2 c. milk or cream
1 head cabbage
3/4 c. cocktail peanuts

Combine eggs, sugar, vinegar and salt in a double boiler. Stir and cook slowly until mixture thickens. Remove from heat and cool; add milk. Shred cabbage and when sauce is completely cool; pour over cabbage. Toss to coat, add peanuts.

Make a heart-in-hand garland for your tree this year using natural parchment paper!

Bread & Butter Pickles

April Hale
Worcester, NY

This recipe came from my husband's grandmother. Every time we would go visit Grandma I would snitch a jar of pickles from her and eat the whole jar! Bread and butter pickles are a favorite recipe of mine...it's my way of remembering all the wonderful times I had with my husband's grandma and mom.

12 6-in. cucumbers
5 medium onions
1/2 c. salt
2 c. water

2 c. vinegar
1-1/2 c. sugar
1-1/2 t. mustard seed
1 t. celery seed

Wash vegetables, cutting cucumbers into 1/2-inch slices without paring. Peel onion and slice into 1/4-inch slices. Place layers of sliced vegetables alternately in a large bowl with salt. Let stand 3 hours. Drain and rinse well with cold water. Mix water, vinegar, sugar, mustard seed and celery seed in a large kettle. Bring to a boil, stirring until sugar is dissolved. Add drained cucumbers and onions and boil 5 minutes. Pour into hot, sterilized jars and seal immediately. Yield: 3 quarts.

Arrange your large cookie cutters on a tray and fill them with nuts or mints.

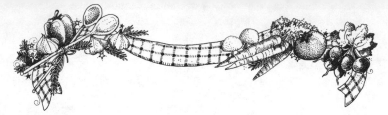

Holiday Sweet Potatoes

Gay Barnhart
Ashley, OH

A must for your holiday table!

23-oz. can sweet potatoes,
   mashed and drained
1/2 t. salt
1/4 c. butter

2 eggs, beaten
1/2 c. sugar
1/4 t. cinnamon
1/4 t. nutmeg

Mix ingredients together and place in a baking dish. Sprinkle topping over top.

Topping:

1/4 c. margarine, melted
3 T. flour

1/2 c. pecans, chopped
3/4 c. brown sugar

Crumble topping ingredients together and sprinkle over potato mixture. Bake at 350 degrees for 30 minutes.

Use spring-type clothespins to keep your strands of lights in place! Simply spray paint them green and let dry.

Delectable Desserts

Yum!

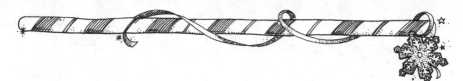

Amish Apple Pie

Mary Murray
Gooseberry Patch

 *An Ohio favorite.*

1 c. sour cream
1 egg
3/4 c. sugar
2 T. all-purpose flour
1/4 t. salt

1 t. vanilla
2-1/2 c. Granny Smith or
    Jonagold apples, peeled and
    diced

Beat sour cream and egg, add sugar, flour, salt and vanilla, combining until smooth. Stir in apples. Bake at 400 degrees for 25 minutes. Remove from oven and top with crumb topping.

Crumb Topping:

1/2 c. brown sugar
1/3 c. all-purpose flour

1/4 c. butter
1 t. cinnamon

Combine crumb topping ingredients and mix until crumbly. Remove pie, spoon crumb topping on and bake an additional 20 minutes. Serves 8.

Steamed Chocolate Pudding

Nancy Campbell
Bellingham, WA

Christmas day at my grandmother and grandfather's house was always filled with family, presents, games and an ample mid-afternoon dinner. We usually had roast beef, several vegetables, hot rolls, pickles, olives and a choice of desserts. She made the pudding in an old fluted tin pudding mold. When she died, my mother gave the tin to me, one of my treasured possessions.

1 egg	1-3/4 c. all-purpose flour, sifted
1 c. sugar	1/2 t. salt
2 T. butter, softened	1/4 t. cream of tartar
2 squares (2-oz.) unsweetened	1/4 t. baking soda
chocolate, melted	1 c. milk

Beat first four ingredients together, mixing well. Sift flour, salt, cream of tartar and soda together; combine with egg mixture. Slowly add in milk. Pour into a greased one-quart mold and steam for 3 hours. Serve with hard sauce.

Hard Sauce:

1/3 c. butter, softened	1 T. cream
1 c. powdered sugar	1 t. vanilla extract

Cream butter, gradually add in other ingredients, beat until fluffy. Chill until cold, but not hard. Yields 3/4 cup of sauce.

Keep a "Christmas cupboard." As you make special purchases throughout the year, tuck your surprises away there. In December, you'll easily remember where to find them.

flying reindeer

Rum Cake

Julie Edwards
Perkasie, PA

This cake freezes well, so go ahead and bake when you have the time!

1/2 c. walnuts or pecans,
   chopped
1 pkg. instant vanilla pudding
1 pkg. yellow cake mix

1/2 c. light rum
1/2 c. water
1/2 c. vegetable cooking oil
4 eggs

Grease and flour a 10-inch tube pan. Sprinkle nuts on bottom.
Combine pudding and cake mix in a large bowl, add rum, water, oil
and eggs. Mix for 2 to 3 minutes. Pour on top of nuts and bake at 325
degrees for 50 to 60 minutes.

Glaze:

1 c. sugar
1 stick butter or margarine

1/4 c. rum
1/4 c. water

Heat all ingredients together in a saucepan, stirring constantly. Boil 2
to 3 minutes and pour over baked cake while still in pan. Let sit for 30
minutes, remove from pan. Makes 12 servings.

*A quick tree skirt can be made easily from a
curtain valance, and they come in all colors!*

Raspberry Truffle Cheesecake

Deborah Hilton
Oswego, NY

Garnish with whipped cream, raspberries and mint leaves...beautiful!

1-1/2 c. chocolate sandwich
    cookies, crushed (about 18
    cookies)
2 T. butter, melted
4 8-oz. pkgs. cream cheese
1-1/4 c. sugar
3 large eggs

1 c. sour cream
1 t. almond extract
2 6-oz. pkgs. chocolate chips
1/3 c. seedless raspberry
    preserves
1/4 c. whipping cream

For crust, combine cookies and butter. Press into a bottom of a 9-inch springform pan. To prepare the filling, combine 3 packages of cream cheese with sugar, mixing at medium speed until well blended. Add eggs, one at a time, mixing after each. Blend in sour cream and extract. Pour over crust. Melt one package of chocolate chips and combine with remaining package of cream cheese. Add preserves and mix well. Drop rounded tablespoonfuls of chocolate cream cheese batter over plain batter. Do not swirl! Bake at 325 degrees for one hour and 20 minutes.

Let cool and remove from pan. To prepare topping, melt remaining chocolate chips with whipping cream over low heat, stirring until smooth. Spread over cheese-cake and let some drizzle over the sides. Chill for 4 hours. Serves 12 to 14.

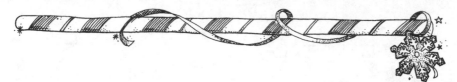

Sweet Potato Pudding

Hannah Gillenwater
Rogersville, TN

A recipe from hardworking mountain folks in the hills of Tennessee! A family tradition coming from my maternal grandfather's family who lived in Cloud's Creek in Hawkins County.

1 stick margarine
4 large white sweet potatoes,
   grated
1 qt. milk
3 t. nutmeg

1 t. ginger
3 T. all-purpose flour
1-1/2 c. brown sugar
1 c. sugar
4 eggs, beaten

Melt margarine in a 13"x9" pan. Add other ingredients, mix well. Bake in 300 degree oven for 2 hours or 250 degree oven for 2-1/2 hours, stirring every 30 minutes. When done, pack into a loaf pan or make a round mound so it can be sliced. Refrigerate. Can be served either cold or warm. Can also be made 2 to 3 days before serving.

Make lacy snowflakes for your windows! Use pretty paper doilies, white poster paint and a sponge. Tape your doilies to a pane of glass, apply water-soluble paint with a sponge, then gently remove doilies. Best of all, these 'snowflakes' wipe off with ease!

Spicy Pumpkin Cheesecake

Sharon Hall
Gooseberry Patch

Forget about calories and enjoy!

1 egg yolk
1 graham cracker pie crust, extra large
2 8-oz. pkg. cream cheese, softened
1/2 to 3/4 c. sugar
2 eggs
16-oz. can pumpkin
1-1/2 t. cinnamon
1/2 t. ginger
1/4 t. cloves
Garnish: 8 oz. whipped topping pecan halves, toasted

Beat egg yolk and brush on crust. Bake at 350 degrees for 5 minutes, then set aside. In a large mixing bowl, beat cream cheese, sugar and eggs at medium speed until smooth. Add pumpkin and remaining spices, continue mixing until well blended. Spoon into pie crust and bake at 350 degrees for 40 to 45 minutes or until set. Cool and refrigerate several hours or overnight. Garnish with whipped topping and toasted pecan halves.

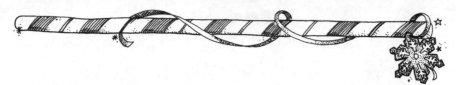

Julegrød

Kimberley Fisher
Cambridge, NY

We have had this Danish Christmas rice pudding tradition in our family for generations. Julegrød is served as the first course at Christmas Eve or Christmas dinner, when the family is together. The person finding the whole almond in their rice pudding will have good luck, and also gets a special treat!

2 c. rice
6 c. milk
1 t. salt
1 c. heavy cream

1 whole almond
cinnamon
sugar

Cook rice and milk on medium-low heat for an hour, stirring often with a wooden spoon. Remove from heat and stir in salt, heavy cream and whole almond. Serve warm in small dishes; top with sprinkles of cinnamon and sugar.

Use plastic cookie cutters dipped in paint to stamp designs onto napkins and placemats.

Noel Ice Cream Cups

Sue Major
Marblehead, OH

A favorite with the kiddie crowd!

1 qt. vanilla ice cream, softened
1/4 c. pecans, toasted and
   chopped
2 T. red and green maraschino
   cherries

1 t. vanilla extract
1/2 t. almond extract
1/2 c . candy-coated chocolates,
   chopped

In a medium bowl combine the ice cream, pecans, cherries and extracts, mixing well. Fold in candy-coated chocolates, reserving some for garnish. Spoon into paper-lined muffin cups and freeze for 30 minutes. Before serving, sprinkle with chopped candy-coated chocolates. Makes 8 to 10 servings.

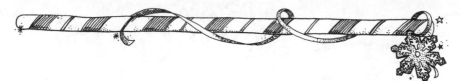

Cream Puff Cake

Vanessa Scutchall
Hopewell, PA

Rich and creamy...serves a whole crowd.

Crust:

1 c. water
1 stick margarine

1 c. flour
4 eggs

Bring water and margarine to a boil, reduce heat and stir in flour until it pulls away from the sides of the pan. Remove from heat and stir in eggs, one at a time. Bake in a preheated 400 degree oven for 15 to 20 minutes in a 13"x9" cake pan. Bake until bubbly and golden brown.

Filling:

8-oz. pkg. cream cheese, room
   temperature
5-oz. box instant vanilla
   pudding

2-1/2 c. cold milk
1 small container whipped
   topping

Mix cream cheese and dry pudding; slowly add milk. Batter will be thick, but smooth. Spread on crust, top with whipped topping. Let chill overnight or at least 2 hours. Serves 15.

Decorate with natural items such as beeswax ornaments, berries, mini oval Shaker boxes, homespun fabrics, dried flower bundles and tiny straw hats to give your tree a simple Shaker look.

Persimmon Cake

Mike Rawl
Jacksonville, FL

A holiday recipe from the deep South.

1-1/2 c. shortening
2-1/2 c. sugar
3 eggs
2-1/2 c. all-purpose flour
2 t. soda
1/2 t. salt

2 t. allspice or pumpkin spice
3 t. cinnamon
2 c. ripe persimmons, peeled and
   mashed
2 c. pecans, chopped
2 c. raisins or dates

Cream shortening and sugar; add eggs. Sift dry ingredients together and add to creamed mixture. Fold in persimmons, pecans and raisins. Pour into greased tube or bundt pan. Bake at 300 degrees for 1-1/2 to 2 hours. Serves 12 to 15.

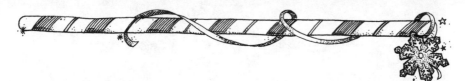

Cranberry Pudding

Jo Baker
Litchfield, IL

Something different for your turkey dinner.

1 c. sugar
2 egg yolks
1 T. butter
1 c. milk

2 c. cranberries, raw
2 c. flour
1 t. baking powder

Combine sugar, egg yolks and butter, stirring well. Add milk and cranberries. Sift together flour and baking powder, then add to mixture. Bake for 45 minutes in a 325 degree oven. Serve warm with pudding sauce.

Pudding Sauce:

1/2 c. sugar
1/2 c. water
1 T. butter

1 t. vinegar
1 t. flour
2 t. vanilla

Heat sugar, water and butter until butter melts. Remove from heat and thicken with flour and small amount of water. Add vinegar and return to stove; boil until thick. Add vanilla when cool.

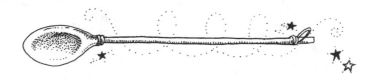

Make a mitten garland! Using jute and wooden clothespins, clip a mitten (one from each family member) to hang on the garland. Terrific to fill with tiny treats throughout the holiday season! Need stuffer ideas? Small packs of hot cocoa, peppermint candies, tiny toys, or even bright, shiny pennies.

Chocolate Chip Cheesecake

Jackie Hoover
Newark, OH

Enjoy the deep, rich chocolate crust.

24 chocolate sandwich cookies,
    crushed
4 T. butter, melted
3 8-oz. pkgs. cream cheese
1 can sweetened condensed milk

3 eggs
1 c. mini chocolate chips
1 T. flour
1 t. vanilla

Mix cookies and butter together and pat into a 9-inch springform pan. Beat remaining ingredients together and pour on top of crust. Bake at 300 degrees until firm, about one hour. Cool, then refrigerate.

For true country spirit, decorate your tree with tiny American flags this year. (Stock up after the 4th of July when you can purchase them readily.)

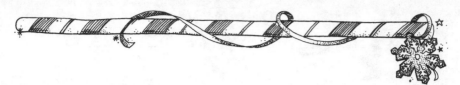

Pistachio-Pineapple Pops

Annie Wolfe
Gooseberry Patch

My kids love this easy treat!

5-oz. box pistachio pudding
1 lb. 14-oz can crushed
   pineapple

9-oz. container whipped topping
1/2 c. walnuts, crushed

In a large bowl combine pudding, pineapple and whipped topping.
Add walnuts and combine well. Place paper cupcake holders in pans
and fill two-thirds full. Insert a wooden ice cream stick into each cup.
Place in freezer until solid. When ready to serve, peel away paper cups.

A quick and easy craft...hot glue two
candy canes together; add a bow and a
jingle bell and hang on the tree.

Creamy Amaretto Cheesecake

Judy Borecky
Escondido, CA

An elegant dessert for a special occasion.

1-1/4 c. coconut or vanilla wafer
  cookies, finely crushed

1/2 c. almonds, ground
6 T. butter, melted

Mix well and press into the bottom and sides of a lightly buttered 8-inch springform pan. Bake in a 350 degree oven until done.

Filling:

3 8-oz. pkgs. cream cheese,
   softened
1 c. sugar
1/4 t. salt

1/2 t. almond extract
1 c. sour cream
3 large eggs
1/4 c. amaretto liqueur

Beat cream cheese in a large bowl until smooth. Add sugar, salt and almond extract. Continue to beat until light and fluffy, about 3 minutes. Beat in sour cream. Add eggs one at a time, beating after each addition and scraping down the sides of the bowl. Slowly beat in the amaretto. Continue to beat at medium speed until well blended, about 3 to 4 minutes. Pour on top of crust and bake at 350 degrees for one hour and 10 minutes or until golden and set. Turn off oven, leaving oven door slightly open. Let cake bake for one to 2 hours. Remove from oven, cover with foil and refrigerate overnight.

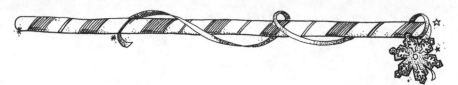

Candy Bar Cake

Charlotte Wolfe
Ft. Lauderdale, FL

Warning! Extremely rich!

8 chocolate-covered nougat
   candy bars
2 sticks butter
2 c. sugar
4 eggs

2-1/2 c. flour
1/2 t. soda
1-1/4 c. buttermilk
1 c. pecans, chopped

Melt candy bars and one stick of butter. Cream sugar and one stick of butter, add eggs, then combine with candy bar mixture. In a separate bowl, alternately combine flour, soda and buttermilk; blend well. Add candy and buttermilk mixtures together, mixing well, then add pecans. Bake in a tube pan at 325 degrees for one hour and 10 minutes. Ice when cool.

Icing:

2-1/2 c. sugar
1 c. evaporated milk
6-oz. pkg. semi-sweet chocolate
   chips

1 c. marshmallow cream
1 stick butter

Combine all ingredients and cook to soft ball stage. Add chocolate chips, marshmallow cream and butter. Stir until completely melted.

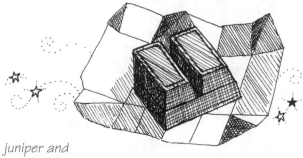

Combine fresh rosebuds, juniper and holly for a romantic holiday wreath.

Peanut Butter Pound Cake

Charlotte Wolfe
Ft. Lauderdale, FL

Delicious without the frosting, too!

1 c. butter
2 c. sugar
1 c. light brown sugar, packed
1/2 c. creamy peanut butter
5 eggs
1 T. vanilla

3 c. cake flour
1/2 t. baking powder
1/2 t. salt
1/4 t. baking soda
1 c. whipping cream, or whole
    milk

Cream butter and sugar until fluffy. Add brown sugar and peanut butter; continue to beat thoroughly. Add eggs, one at at time, beating well after each addition; add vanilla and blend well. Sift together the dry ingredients and add alternately with whipping cream or milk. Pour into a very large tube pan that's been lightly greased and floured. Bake at 325 degrees for one hour or until it tests done. Frost, if desired, with peanut butter frosting.

Frosting:

1/2 stick butter
dash salt
1 oz. milk
2 eggs

1/3 c. creamy peanut
    butter
1 box powdered sugar

Combine all ingredients and beat until smooth.

Chocolate House

Debbie Parker
Gooseberry Patch

Entertain your guests with flaming chocolate!

chocolate coating, chopped into
   small pieces
2 pts. strawberries, or other
   seasonal fruit

2 chocolate cups
10 oz. 151 rum

Line two 13" x 9" jelly roll pans (or cookie sheets with an edge) with wax paper. Melt the chocolate coating over a double boiler, taking care not to overheat the chocolate because it can become very dry. When chocolate is melted, pour onto your baking sheets lined with wax paper. When chocolate has cooled and is hard, use your favorite gingerbread house template for cutouts. Remember to leave a chimney hole in your chocolate roof to pour the flaming rum in. Melt down the "scrap" pieces of chocolate that will be used like glue to stick the house together. Set a heat and fireproof tray on trivets to protect your tabletop. Start by assembling one side of the house with the back of the house. Use melted chocolate to adhere the seams together. Attach the opposite side of the house to the back piece. Within seconds these three sides should be able to stand up on their own. Next attach the front of the house to complete all four sides. If you have a doorway cut-out in your template pattern, use your melted chocolate to attach a cooled, small piece of chocolate inside the doorway. This will keep the rum from seeping out the doorway. Using any leftover melted chocolate, seal the inside edges of the house that are touching the tray. This will help keep the rum from leaking under the house. To make chocolate cups, brush melted chocolate inside two miniature muffin size muffin liners; allow to cool. When solid, remove liner. Place both chocolate cups inside the house and fill them with rum, fill the inside of the house with strawberries. Using melted chocolate, adhere the roof to the top of the house. Now, the house is ready to be "burned down." Using caution, fill a long-handled metal ladle with 3 ounces of rum. Turn down the lights and carefully light the rum in your ladle with a match. Pour lighted rum into the open chimney in your house. The rum inside will ignite, increasing your flame. Watch as your house melts all over the strawberries! Use two serving scoops to help with the breaking up of your house. Serve over your favorite ice cream.

Miniature Cheesecakes

Beth Warner
Delaware, OH

Vanilla wafers speed up this recipe!

3 8-oz. pkgs. cream cheese,
   softened
1 c. sugar

6 eggs
1-1/2 t. vanilla
1 box miniature vanilla wafers

Combine cream cheese and sugar, add eggs, one at a time, beating well after each; add vanilla. Place one vanilla wafer in the bottom of a cup-lined mini-muffin tin. Pour mixture on top of wafer, filling cup 3/4 full. Bake 20 to 25 minutes at 300 degrees. Immediately add topping and bake an additional 10 minutes.

Topping:

1 pt. sour cream
1-1/2 t. vanilla
1/2 c. sugar

Combine ingredients, mixing well.

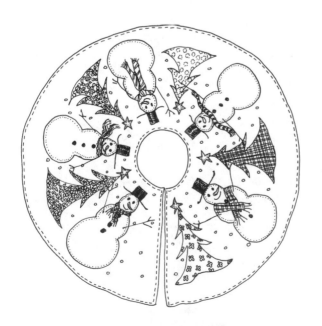

Store your Christmas tree skirt with sachets made of lavender buds and cedar chips...keeps it smelling fresh.

Eclair Squares

Ginny Pereda
Roebling, NJ

Creamy and delicious!

1 c. water	1 c. flour
1/2 c. butter	4 eggs, beaten

Prepare the dough first by boiling water and butter, stirring until margarine is melted. Turn the heat off, but leave the saucepan on the burner. Add flour, stirring until smooth, then add eggs, mixing well. Spread in a greased 17"x11" jelly roll pan. Bake at 400 degrees for 30 to 35 minutes or until golden. Cool and smooth out any air bubbles. Top cooled crust with filling.

Filling:

2 pkgs. instant vanilla pudding	8-oz. pkg. cream cheese
4 c. cold milk	8-oz. container whipped topping

Prepare pudding using 3 cups of milk. Blend cream cheese and remaining cup of milk in a blender. Add to pudding mixture. Spread on cooled crust and let set 10 minutes in the refrigerator. Top with whipped topping and drizzle with chocolate syrup.

Cookies
Cookies
Cookies

Merry-Maker Sugar Cookies

LaRayne Cummons
Lakeview, OH

The most fun to decorate at cookie-baking parties.

1-1/2 c. powdered sugar
1 stick butter
1 stick margarine
1 egg
1-1/2 t. vanilla
2-1/2 c. flour

1 t. baking soda
1 t. cream of tartar
food coloring
sprinkles
colored sugar

Mix sugar, butter and margarine. Add egg and vanilla, mixing thoroughly. Mix dry ingredients together and blend into sugar mixture. Divide dough into parts, working in food coloring. Wrap each section in wax paper and refrigerate until well chilled. Remove from refrigerator and roll on a lightly floured board to 1/8-inch thickness. Using your favorite cutters, cut out shapes and decorate with sprinkles or colored sugar. Bake on lightly greased cookie sheet for 7 to 8 minutes or until lightly golden.

Flour your cookie cutters to help keep them from sticking! Since cookie cutters can rust, dry them completely, then use a hair dryer to remove all water. You can even flour them again and store in a plastic bag.

Fresh Apple Bars

LaRayne Cummons
Lakeview, OH

Try these with walnuts or almonds.

3 eggs
1-3/4 c. sugar
1 c. oil
2 c. flour
1/2 t. salt

1 t. baking soda
1/2 t. cinnamon
2 c. sliced apples
1 c. nuts
powdered sugar for topping

Preheat oven to 350 degrees. Beat eggs, sugar and oil together. Add sifted dry ingredients. Fold in apples and nuts and pour into a greased and floured 13"x9" pan. Bake 40 to 45 minutes. When done, sprinkle top with powdered sugar and cut into bars.

Best Pecan Brittle

Gay Barnhart
Ashley, OH

A good "munchie" while you're wrapping gifts!

1 c. sugar
1/2 c. dark corn syrup
1/2 stick butter

1" square of paraffin
2 c. pecan halves
2 t. soda

Microwave sugar, syrup and butter 3 minutes on high. Stir in paraffin and allow to melt. Add nuts and mix well. Microwave on high setting for 10 to 12 minutes, checking nuts several times to make sure they don't burn. Add soda, quickly stir and pour onto greased surface. Cool and break into pieces. Store in an airtight container.

Variations:

Substitute light brown sugar and maple syrup for sugar and corn syrup. Also try peanuts, almonds, cashews, walnuts and coconut combinations.

Grandma Weiser's English Toffee

Deb Weiser
Gooseberry Patch

A favorite family recipe.

1 c. butter
1 c. sugar
1 T. light corn syrup

2 T. water
1 c. almonds
6 oz. chocolate chips

Combine all ingredients in a heavy pan except nuts and chocolate chips. Stirring constantly, cook until candy thermometer reads 300 degrees or until candy is thick. Spread on buttered cookie sheet, then sprinkle with chocolate chips. Spread chips evenly until melted and top is completely covered. Sprinkle with almond pieces and refrigerate to set. Crack into pieces before serving.

Serve Christmas petit-fours on a lovely silver platter...an elegant treat.

Grandma Horger's Kifli

Carol Bull
Gooseberry Patch

My grandmother was a first-generation German-American who believed Christmas wasn't Christmas without 20 or 30 different types of cookies. She would bake for weeks and store them all in big suit boxes up in the attic. When we would go to her house for a visit, she would say, "Let me get down a few cookies," and down would come box after box of wonderful baked treasures. Grandma's health failed, but before she passed away I spent a Saturday going through her recipe box and copying all the recipes that would keep her cookie-baking legacy alive for my family. One of her specialities was a recipe for nut-filled rolls she called "Kifli." She made dozens of these each Christmas to give to her family and friends. My mother and I took up the tradition, and now we make these each holiday.

6 c. flour	dash of salt
1 c. butter	1 t. lemon rind, grated
2 cakes yeast	3/4 or 1 c. milk
1/2 c. warm water	sugar
6 egg yolks	

In a large bowl mix together flour and butter. In a separate bowl mix yeast, water, egg yolks, salt, lemon rind and milk. Combine the two mixtures together and place dough in a wet towel in the refrigerator for 2-1/2 hours. Remove part of the dough and shape into walnut-sized balls. Roll in sugar on a board to make 2-1/2 inch rounds. Spread with filling, then roll into crescents. Place on a baking sheet and bake at 350 degrees until light brown.

Aunt Velma's Kifli Filling:

1 pt. milk	1/2 t. salt
1/4 lb. butter	2 lbs. nuts, ground
6 c. sugar	2 eggs

Scald milk, add butter sugar and salt. Add nuts, then eggs and mix well. Cook slowly until it reaches a spreading consistency.

Snowy Black Walnut Cookies

Marilyn Briggs
Albion, NY

A great, chewy texture.

1/2 c. margarine
1-1/2 c. sugar
3 eggs, beaten
1 t. vanilla
3-1/2 c. flour
1 t. baking soda in 2 T. boiling
    water

1 lb. dates, chopped
1 c. black walnuts, chopped
1/2 c. maraschino cherries,
    chopped
powdered sugar

Cream margarine and sugar, add eggs and vanilla. Mix in part of the flour with fruit and nuts. Add soda and water, mix well, add remaining flour. Drop by rounded teaspoonfuls onto a greased cookie sheet. Bake at 425 degrees for 10 to 15 minutes. While still warm, roll in powdered sugar.

Sour Cream Sugar Cookies

Marie Christensen
Flint, MI

A special recipe over 100 years old!

2 eggs, beaten
2 c. sugar
3/4 c. shortening
1 c. sour cream
1/2 t. vanilla

3/4 c. flour
2 t. baking powder
1 t. nutmeg
1 t. baking soda
4 c. flour

Combine eggs, sugar, shortening, sour cream and vanilla, mixing well. Sift together 3/4 cup flour, baking powder, nutmeg and baking soda and add to creamed mixture, blending well. Add 4 cups of flour, stir well and roll out. Cut shapes with your favorite cookie cutters. Bake on an ungreased cookie sheet at 350 degrees for 8 to 10 minutes or until very lightly browned.

Lemon Bites

Gen Hellums
Freer, TX

No one will guess how easy!

18.25-oz. pkg. lemon-flavored
   cake mix
1 egg

4-oz. container non-dairy
   whipped topping
1/2 c. powdered sugar

Preheat oven to 350 degrees. In a large bowl, combine cake mix, egg and whipped topping; batter will be very stiff. Drop by teaspoons into powdered sugar. Roll into one-inch balls, using the sugar to keep the dough from sticking to your hands. Place balls of dough 2 inches apart on a greased baking sheet. Bake for 10 to 12 minutes, or until light brown on the underside. Transfer to a wire rack to cool. Store in an airtight container. Yields 6 dozen cookies.

Cinnamon Crunch Bars

Gen Hellums
Freer, TX

Keep on hand for the grandchildren.

12 cinnamon graham crackers,
   2-1/2"x4-3/4"
2 c. walnuts or pecans, chopped

1 c. butter
1 c. brown sugar, firmly packed
1/2 t. cinnamon

Preheat oven to 400 degrees. In the bottom of a greased 15"x10" jelly roll pan, arrange graham crackers in a single layer with sides touching. Sprinkle nuts evenly over crackers. In a small heavy saucepan, combine butter, brown sugar, and cinnamon. Stirring constantly, cook over medium heat until sugar dissolves and mixture begins to boil. Continue to boil syrup for 3 minutes longer without stirring; pour over crackers. Bake 8 to 10 minutes or until bubbly and slightly darker around the edges. Cool completely in pan; break into pieces. Store in an airtight container. Yields about 1-1/2 pounds of candy.

Gingerbread Men

Nancy Campbell
Bellingham, WA

For many years it has been the tradition at our house for me to bake gingerbread men. The recipe makes 6 dozen cookies, so I have a tabletop full of them when I'm through! Each man is carefully decorated with simple white icing and cinnamon red hot "buttons." Long after my children's friends had grown up, they still came around at Christmastime for a gingerbread man!

1/3 c. shortening
1 c. light brown sugar, packed
1-1/2 c. light molasses
2/3 c. cold water
6 c. all-purpose flour
2 t. baking soda

1/2 t. salt
1 t. allspice
1 t. ginger
1 t. cloves
1 t. cinnamon

Mix first four ingredients together until thoroughly combined. Sift together dry ingredients and stir into molasses mixture. Chill dough overnight. When ready to bake, roll 1/4-inch thick and cut with gingerbread man cookie cutter. Place on lightly greased cookie sheet; bake at 350 degrees for 15 minutes. Yields 6 dozen.

Antique sifters make perfect display settings for sugar cookies and gingerbread men.

Pecan Bars

Delores Berg
Selah, WA

These are too good for words!

1/2 c. butter
1/2 c. sugar
1 t. lemon peel

1/2 t. vanilla
1-1/4 c. flour

Beat butter on high for 30 seconds. Add sugar, lemon peel and vanilla. Beat in flour. Pat in the bottom of a 13"x9" pan and bake at 350 degrees for 15 minutes. Reduce oven to 325 degrees, remove crust and pour in filling.

Filling:

1/3 c. butter
1/2 c. brown sugar
1/3 c. honey

3 T. sugar
1-3/4 c. pecans, chopped
1/4 c. whipping cream

Combine first four filling ingredients in a saucepan and cook over medium heat until it comes to a boil. Remove from heat and stir in pecans and cream. Pour over crust and bake 25 minutes. Cut into bars when cool.

Remember candy canes, pocket games, and small trinkets for stocking stuffers!

Maple Bars

Phyllis M. Peters
Three Rivers, MI

A Christmas favorite for 40 years!

2 eggs, beaten
2/3 c. vegetable oil
1 c. flour
1 c. sugar

1 c. walnuts
2 t. maple flavoring
1 t. baking powder

Combine all ingredients and place into a greased 9"x9" baking pan. Bake at 350 degrees for 30 minutes, being careful not to over-bake. Cool and cut into bars, then roll in powdered sugar. Yield: 16 to 20 bars.

Simply Fudge

Wendy Lee Paffenroth
Pine Island, NY

Perhaps the world's fudgiest fudge.

18-oz. pkg. semi-sweet
    chocolate morsels
1 can sweetened condensed milk
dash of salt

1-1/2 t. vanilla
1/2 t. almond extract
1/2 c. walnuts, chopped,
    optional

In a heavy sauce pot, melt the chips over a very low flame, stirring often to prevent burning. When smooth, pour in the sweetened milk and stir. Remove from heat and add a dash of salt and extracts; mix quickly, it becomes stiff very quickly. Stir in walnuts if desired and spread into a 9"x9" pan lined with wax paper. Place in the refrigerator for at least 2 hours, then turn onto a wooden board, and cut into small pieces.

Kentucky Bourbon Balls

Mary Folsom
Lakeland, FL

♥ *Dad's been making these at Christmastime for years;*
it's a family favorite!

2 c. walnuts, chopped
10 T. bourbon, divided
2 sticks butter, softened

2 lb. powdered sugar
1 lb. semi-sweet candy coating
   chocolate
♥

Combine walnuts and 6 tablespoons bourbon well and let stand
overnight. Cream butter, sugar and 4 tablespoons of bourbon, blending
well. Add walnut and bourbon mixture and chill at least one hour. Roll
into one-inch balls. Place balls on wax paper-lined cookie sheet; chill
again for one hour. Melt chocolate slowly in a double boiler, spoon
over balls, chill. These are equally good made with rum.

Decorate your kitchen with an old-fashioned feather tree, dressed in a
combination of new and old ornaments. Stand it atop an old butcher block!

Chocolate-Covered Cherry Cookies

Tammy Barnum
Portland, TN

One of our favorites.

1-1/2 c. flour
1/2 c. unsweetened cocoa
   powder
1/4 t. salt
1/4 t. baking powder
1/4 t. baking soda
1/2 c. butter, softened
1 c. sugar

1 egg
1-1/2 t. vanilla
21-oz. can cherry pie filling,
   reserving 4 t. of filling sauce
6-oz. pkg. semi-sweet chocolate
   chips
1/2 c. sweetened condensed
   milk

Add first five ingredients together in a large bowl. In a separate bowl, beat together butter and sugar until fluffy. Add egg and vanilla; beat well. Gradually add dry ingredients to creamed mixture; beat until well blended. Shape into one-inch balls. Place on ungreased cookie sheet; press down center of dough with thumb. Place a cherry in the center of each cookie. In a small saucepan, combine chocolate chips and sweetened condensed milk; heat until chocolate is melted. Stir in 4 teaspoons of the sauce from pie filling. Spoon about a teaspoon of frosting over each cherry, spreading to cover cherry. Bake in a 350 degree oven about 10 minutes or until done. Remove to wire rack to cool. Makes 48 cookies.

Send a few tins of Christmas cookies to your local nursing home or hospital to brighten someone's holidays!

Caramel Popcorn Balls

Liz VanBuren
Sidney Center, NY

Pile them in a pottery bowl for holiday snacking!

8 c. popped popcorn
3/4 c. sugar
3/4 c. brown sugar, packed
1/2 c. light corn syrup

1/2 c. water
1 t. white vinegar
1/4 t. salt
3/4 c. butter

Measure popcorn into a large bowl. Combine sugars, corn syrup, water, vinegar and salt in a saucepan. Heat to boiling over medium heat, stirring frequently. Cook, stirring constantly, until mixture reaches 260 degrees on a candy thermometer. Reduce heat to low and stir in butter until melted. Pour syrup in a thin stream over popped corn, stirring until popcorn is thoroughly coated. Cool slightly. Butter hands, and being careful, as the mixture is still very warm, shape into 3 or 4-inch balls and place on wax paper. When completely cool, wrap individually in clear and colored plastic wrap and tie ends with curled or decorative ribbon. Makes one to two dozen, depending on the size.

Wrap popcorn balls in colorful plastic wrap and tie with a festive bow. Stack them in a basket near your door for quick gifts for the mailman, paper carrier, or strolling carolers!

Oatmeal Caramelitas

Tammy Barnum
Portland, TN

A great recipe from Mom, of course!

1 c. flour
1 c. quick oats
3/4 c. brown sugar
1/2 t. baking soda
1/4 t. salt

3/4 c. butter, melted
1 c. chocolate chips
1/2 c. nuts, chopped
3/4 c. caramel ice cream topping
3 T. flour

Grease bottom and sides of a 9-inch square pan. Combine one cup flour, oats, brown sugar, soda, salt and butter in a large bowl to form crumbs. Press half of the crumbs into the bottom of the pan; bake at 350 degrees for 10 minutes. Sprinkle the chocolate chips and nuts over the baked crust. Mix the caramel topping and the flour together and drizzle over the chips and the nuts. Sprinkle remaining crumbs over caramel topping and bake at 350 degrees for 15 to 20 minutes, or until golden brown. Chill bars for easy cutting. Makes about 15 bars.

Tuck small trees into corners or unusual places. They'll be "discovered" by family and friends!

Honey Nut Christmas Cookies

Michele Grippa
Aliquippa, PA

These are reminiscent of baklava, but easier to make! Stand back and take the compliments, these are good!

2 c. flour
pinch salt
1 c. cold butter
8-oz. pkg. cream cheese
1 c. walnuts

1/4 c. sugar
6 T. honey
1 t. butter, melted
1/2 t. cinnamon

Combine flour and salt in a large bowl. Cut up butter and cream cheese and add to flour. With pastry blender or 2 knives, cut in until blended to the consistency of coarse grain. Divide in half; shape dough into 2 balls, wrap and refrigerate for one hour.

Grind nuts with sugar in a food processor, then transfer to a bowl. Stir in honey, butter and cinnamon. Preheat oven to 325 degrees and grease two cookie sheets. On a well-floured surface, roll one dough ball 1/8-inch thick and cut into circles using a 2-inch cookie cutter or a floured glass. Place one teaspoon of nut and honey filling on half the circles, top with remaining circles making a sandwich. Press edges with a fork to seal. Transfer to cookie sheets and bake 22 to 25 minutes or until golden. Repeat with remaining dough scraps and filling.

baskets full of goodies

Pets are a part of the family, too! Your friends will be touched if you remember their pet with a small gift of dog biscuits or a catnip toy.

Nutmeg Logs

Donna Kincaid
Clarksboro, NJ

You can shape these into rainbows and dip in multicolored sprinkles.

1 c. butter or margarine,
    softened
2 t. vanilla
1 t. almond extract
3/4 c. sugar
1 egg

3 c. flour
1-1/2 t. nutmeg
1/4 t. salt
6 oz. chocolate chips
chocolate jimmies or sprinkles

Cream butter with flavorings. Gradually beat in sugar, then blend in egg. Mix together flour, nutmeg and salt. Add to butter mixture and mix well. Divide into 14 equal pieces. On a sugared board, shape each piece into a roll 12 inches long and 1/2 inch in diameter. Cut into 2-inch lengths and put on greased cookie sheets. Bake in a preheated 350 degree oven for 12 minutes. When cool, dip both ends in melted chocolate chips, then in jimmies. Makes about 7 dozen.

Sparkly snowflakes! Hang paper snowflakes (embellished with thin fancy ribbons and iridescent glitter) in each pane of your windows.

Christmas Candy

Jennifer Janes
Lima, NY

When I was younger my mother and her girlfriend would get together before Christmas every year to make this delicious candy. Even with seven kids running around, they still managed to make several batches! It's been a tradition for many years.

3-3/4 c. sugar
1-1/4 c. light corn syrup
1 c. water

1 box powdered sugar
red and green food coloring
your favorite flavoring oils

Stir together sugar, corn syrup and water in a saucepan. Boil until mixture comes to 300 degrees, the hard crack stage. Cover at least 3 cookie sheets with 3/4 inch of powdered sugar, then run your fingers through the sugar to make gutters. Pour candy into the gutters and, using a fork, rake a little of the powdered sugar over the candy. Cut candy while it is still hot and before it gets solid to prevent cracking.

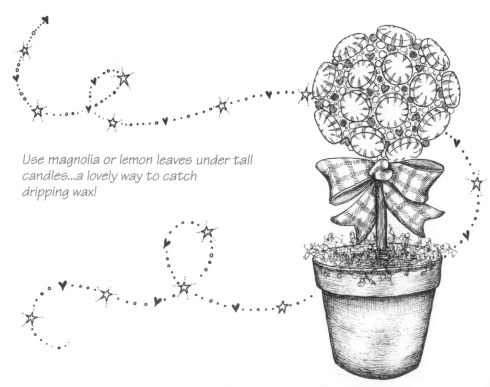

Use magnolia or lemon leaves under tall candles...a lovely way to catch dripping wax!

Butter Gerbachnas

Ginny Pereda
Roebling, NJ

This recipe came from my grandmother's German family. Three generations have made them. Their taste and smell are the essence of Christmas to me.

1 lb. butter
1 lb. powdered sugar
5 eggs, beaten

2 lb. flour
1 T. baking powder
1 T. cinnamon

Soften butter and mix with sugar, four eggs and dry ingredients. Chill well, then roll out and cut with your favorite cookie cutters. Brush with a beaten egg and bake in a 350 degree oven until golden.

Sugar Crispies

Peggy Peters
Chittenango, NY

An easy cookie to make with the kids!

1 c. shortening
2 c. sugar
2 eggs
1 c. oil
1/2 t. salt

1 t. vanilla
5 c. flour
2 t. baking soda
2 t. cream of tartar
colored sugar for coating

Cream together shortening, sugar, eggs, oil, salt and vanilla. Sift all dry ingredients and add to creamed mixture. Roll into one-inch balls and roll in sugar. Flatten with a fork and bake at 350 degrees for 10 minutes. Yield: 8 dozen.

Butterscotch Coffee Spice Bars

Barbara Nicol
Marysville, OH

A sweet treat for coffee and conversation!

1 c. brown sugar, packed
1/2 c. shortening
1 egg
1/2 c. hot water
1 t. regular instant coffee
  powder
1-1/2 c. sifted all-purpose flour

1 t. baking powder
1/2 t. baking soda
1/2 t. salt
1/2 t. cinnamon
1 c. butterscotch-flavored
  morsels
1/2 c. nuts, chopped

Combine brown sugar, shortening and egg; beat until creamy. Mix hot water and instant coffee; blend into creamed mixture. Sift together flour, baking powder, baking soda, salt and cinnamon; gradually stir into creamed mixture. Add butterscotch-flavored morsels and chopped nuts; mix well. Spread in greased and floured 13"x9"x2" pan. Bake in 350 degree oven for 20 to 25 minutes. Cool, cut into 3"x1-1/2" bars. Makes about 2 dozen.

When you have family members visiting for the holidays (especially those who live far away), get out the old picture albums, slides and family films! What a joy to reminisce together, laugh and share special memories of childhood and Christmases past!

Holiday Melting Moments

Terri Vanden Bosch
Rock Valley, IA

These are a tradition in the making. They are my 8-year-old daughter Ashley's favorite. Her holiday is not complete without them! I have a batch in the refrigerator right now waiting to be baked for her!

1 c. butter (no substitutes)
1 egg yolk
1 c. plus 1 T. flour
1/8 t. salt

1/2 c. powdered sugar
1/2 c. corn starch
2 T. unsweetened cocoa

Mix butter and egg yolk well. Put all the dry ingredients into a sifter; sift and stir into the butter and egg mixture. Stir well. Cover and chill until firm, one to 2 hours. Make one-inch balls and bake at 375 degrees for 8 to 10 minutes until set but not brown. When cool, frost with frosting and dip tops into crushed candy canes.

Frosting:

1 c. powdered sugar
2 to 4 T. milk
2 T. butter, softened

1 t. vanilla or peppermint extract
crushed candy canes for topping

Stir together all ingredients, adding more milk as necessary to make smooth. Yield: 3-1/2 dozen cute little cookies!

Santa Claus Cookie Pops   *Vickie*

Put one at each place setting or pass them out at a party.

1 c. sugar
1/2 c. shortening
2 T. milk
1 large egg
2 c. all-purpose flour

1 t. baking powder
1/2 t. baking soda
1/2 t. salt
sugar, for dipping glass in

Preheat oven to 400 degrees. Mix sugar, shortening, milk and egg in a large bowl with a wooden spoon. Stir in flour, baking powder, baking soda and salt. Shape dough into 1-1/4 inch balls. Insert one flat wooden ice cream stick into the side of each flattened ball of dough until tip of stick is in the center of the ball. Place balls 2 inches apart on a cookie sheet and flatten with the bottom of a glass dipped in sugar. Bake 8 to 10 minutes or until cookies are light brown. Remove from cookie sheet and cool on a wire rack. Frost when completely cool.

Frosting:

1-1/2 c. powdered sugar
1/2 t. vanilla
2 to 3 T. water
3 T. red sugar
1/2 c. coconut, shredded

30 miniature marshmallows
60 raisins
30 red cinnamon candies
30 wooden ice-cream sticks

Mix powdered sugar, vanilla and water in a small bowl, adding water one teaspoon at a time, until spreadable. Spread frosting on one cookie at a time, then sprinkle red sugar on top third for a hat and coconut on bottom third for a beard. Press on one marshmallow for tassel of hat, 2 raisins for eyes and one cinnamon candy for nose.

Make little bouquets of evergreens tied with tartan plaid ribbons and place one above each place setting at your holiday dinner table.

THE Peanut Butter Bars

Carol Bull
Gooseberry Patch

Many years ago when I was in Elementary School, our "Lunch Lady,"
Mrs. Hopkins, made these for us once a week. The aroma filled the
school as they were baking and we knew we were in store for the
best possible treat. I've never had anything that tasted so good!
Now I make these for my own family and they agree...they are
THE Peanut Butter Bar.

1-1/2 c. + 2 T. butter
3/4 c. peanut butter
1/4 c. light corn syrup
1 c. sugar

2 eggs
1-3/4 c. flour
1 t. salt

Cream butter and peanut butter, add corn syrup, sugar, eggs, flour and
salt. Mix about 5 minutes. Spread in greased 13"x9" pan. Bake at 350
degrees for 25 minutes; watching carefully. Cool, frost, cut into squares.

Icing:

1/4 c. shortening, melted and
    cooled
1/2 c. cocoa
1/4 t. salt

1/3 c. milk
1-1/2 t. vanilla
3-1/2 c. powdered sugar

Combine shortening, cocoa and salt. Add milk and vanilla. Stir in
powdered sugar in three parts; beat well.

Spiked Pecan Brownies

Carol Bull
Gooseberry Patch

4 oz. unsweetened chocolate
1 c. flour
1/4 t. salt
2 t. instant espresso coffee mix
1 t. vanilla
1 c. pecans, coarsely chopped

1 c. semi-sweet chocolate chips
1-1/2 sticks unsalted butter,
   room temperature
1-2/3 c. sugar
4 eggs

Preheat oven to 350 degrees. Grease a 13"x9" pan. Melt chocolate and set aside. Sift together flour and salt. Combine coffee and vanilla in a cup. In a separate bowl, stir together pecans and chips. In a large mixing bowl cream butter, add sugar and continue beating until light and fluffy. Add eggs, one at a time, beating well. Add the melted chocolate and espresso mixture. Fold in flour mixture by hand with a wooden spoon just until moist. Reserving 1/2 cup of nut and chip mixture, gently stir in remaining nuts and chips. Spread batter in pan and top with reserved chip and nut mixture. Bake 22 to 25 minutes or until tooth- pick inserted comes out slightly wet. Cool, cut into squares.

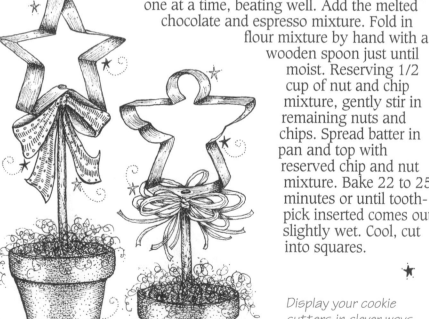

Display your cookie cutters in clever ways when not in use in the kitchen.

Santa Cookies

Lillian S. Terrell
Martha I. Terrell
Dillwyn, VA

Children will love making these cookies to leave out with a glass of milk on Christmas Eve!

sugar cookie dough
white frosting
red decorative sugar
iridescent edible glitter

mini marshmallows
raisins
red hot candies

Using your favorite sugar cookie recipe, prepare cookie dough. Cut with a round cutter and bake according to your recipe. When cool, ice with white frosting. Decorate the top third in a crescent shape, using the red colored sugar to resemble a hat. Place a miniature marshmallow at the top, use raisins for eyes, red hot candy for a nose and iridescent edible glitter for a beard. Santa will be flattered!

Hosting a cookie exchange? Arrange the cookies in all sorts of interesting containers...hat boxes, antique tins, depression glass platters, or a footed cake plate.

Index

APPETIZERS
Apple & Pear-Shaped Cheese Balls, 106
Barb's Crab Canapes, 102
BBQ Sausage Balls, 99
Chicken Gemmies, 103
Crab Meltaways, 98
Herbal Cheese Spread, 60
Holiday Cheese Bell, 96
Honey-Glazed Snack Mix, 54
Hot Crab Dip, 113
Hot Pepper Dip, 101
Mary's Reuben Dip, 103
No-Fat Bean & Salsa Dip, 101
Party Nuts, 66
Pumpkin Dip, 97
Ranch Potato Skins, 108
Salmon Party Log, 100
Sausage Pizza Appetizer, 97
Sausage Swirls, 96
Shrimp Dip, 104
Sweet & Sour Meatballs, 104
Tropical Chicken Wings, 100

BEVERAGES
Brandy Cider Tea, 108
Celebration Punch, 105
Chocolate-Covered Spoons, 62
Christmas Wreath Punch, 107
Coffee Punch, 113
Glöggi, 110
Holiday Grog, 109
Hot Candy Cane, 95
Hot Christmas Punch, 105
Hot Spiced Tea, 58
Rosy Mulled Cider, 112
Sparkling Punch, 110
Vanilla Sugar, 65

BREADS
Banana Muffins, 131
Cheese Danish Coffee Braid, 84
Christmas Tea Ring, 86
Colonial Brown Bread, 126
Crunchy Apple Muffins, 81
Easy Cheese Bread, 126
Eggnog Quick Bread, 88
Elf Muffins, 122
Empire State Muffins, 127
Make-Ahead Dinner Rolls, 124
Mom's Beautiful Babka, 90
Olliebollen (Raisin Bread), 89
Pumpkin Bread, 130
Savory Herb Biscuits, 129
Savory Mini-Bagels, 117
Sourdough French Bread, 119
Sourdough Starter, 118
Woodland Altars Whole Wheat Bread, 115

BREAKFAST
Baked French Toast & Strawberries, 83
Blueberry-Lemon Crepes, 82
Breakfast Cheesecake, 85
Breakfast Sausage & Fruit, 78

CAKES
Apple Cream Cheese Coffee Cake, 92
Candy Bar Cake, 187
Chocolate Chip Cheesecake, 184
Chocolate Jar Cakes, 63
Christmas Almond Pound Cake, 87
Cream Puff Cake, 181
Creamy Amaretto Cheesecake, 186
Grandma's Coffee Cake, 76
Miniature Cheesecakes, 190
Peanut Butter Pound Cake, 188
Persimmon Cake, 182
Raspberry Coffee Cake, 91
Raspberry Truffle Cheesecake, 176
Rum Cake, 175
Spicy Pumpkin Cheesecake, 178

CANDIES & CONFECTIONS
Almond Brittle, 64
Best Pecan Brittle, 194
Christmas Candy, 208
Christmas Crunch, 60
Cranberry Snow Candy, 56
Sugared Nuts, 61
Toffee Delight, 53

CASSEROLES
Asparagus Casserole, 161
Barley Casserole, 160
Curry Chicken Casserole, 151
Deviled Ham Casserole, 75
Scallop Casserole, 137
Spinach Casserole, 161
Sweet Potato Casserole, 164

Index

COOKIES
Butter Gerbachnas, 209
Butterscotch Coffee Spice Bars, 210
Caramel Popcorn Balls, 204
Christmas Meringues, 65
Chocolate-Covered Cherry Cookies, 203
Cinnamon Crunch Bars, 198
Fresh Apple Bars, 194
Holiday Melting Moments, 211
Honey Nut Christmas Cookies, 206
Gingerbread Men, 199
Grandma Horger's Kifli, 196
Grandma Weiser's English Toffee, 195
Kentucky Bourbon Balls, 202
Lemon Bites, 198
Maple Bars, 201
Merry-Maker Sugar Cookies, 193
Nutmeg Logs, 207
Oatmeal Caramelitas, 205
Pecan Bars, 200
Santa Claus Cookie Pops, 212
Santa Cookies, 215
Simply Fudge, 201
Snowy Black Walnut Cookies, 197
Sour Cream Sugar Cookies, 197
Spiked Pecan Brownies, 214
Sugar Crispies, 209
THE Peanut Butter Bars, 213

DESSERTS
Cheese Danish Pastries, 93
Chocolate House, 189
Christmas Kringle, 77
Cinnamon Spirals, 80
Cranberry Pudding, 183
Eclair Squares, 191
Julegrod, 179
Noel Ice Cream Cups, 180
Pistachio-Pineapple Pops, 185
Steamed Chocolate Pudding, 174
Sweet Potato Pudding, 177

EGG DISHES
Sausage & Egg Casserole, 75
Scottish Eggs, 79

MEATS & FISH
Baked Maple Ham, 148
Beef, Pasta & Artichoke Toss, 149
Cranberry-Glazed Pork Roast, 147
Creamy Mushroom & Ham Ravioli, 141
Garlic-Dijon Puff Pastry Ham, 136
Pork Crown Roast with Fruit Glaze, 133
Roast Beef, 138
Shrimp Louis, 111
Tourtiere-Pork Pie, 146

PIES
Amish Apple Pie, 173

POULTRY
Chicken Divan, 150
Creamy Chicken Enchiladas, 142
Glazed Cornish Game Hens, 140
Lemon Deluxe Chicken, 143
Lori's Cabin Chicken, 144
Roast Chicken Dinner, 138
Roast Vermont Turkey, 134
Traditional Christmas Goose, 145

SALADS
Chicken & Shrimp Salad, 159
Cranberry Waldorf Salad, 153
Frosty Cranberry Mold, 156
Fruit Salad with Orange Dressing, 158
Grandma Tilden's Peanut Coleslaw, 169
Pasta with Red Pepper & Broccoli, 168
Taffy Apple Salad, 155
Sesame Seafood Salad, 154
Winter Salad, 157

SAUCES, SPREADS & VINEGARS
Cranberry Lemon Vinegar, 57
Lemon Scallion Vinegar, 57
Microwave Peach Butter, 54
Spicy Orange Butter, 61

SIDES
Bread & Butter Pickles, 170
Chestnut Stuffing, 163
Holiday Spiced Peaches, 165
Holiday Sweet Potatoes, 171
Honey-Orange Carrots, 162
Hot Spiced Fruit, 167
Mashed Potato Soufflé, 162
Mexican Rice, 168
Oyster Stuffing, 160
Pam's Cheese Potatoes, 166
Roasted Redskins Dijon, 167
Sausage Stuffing, 135
Savannah Red Rice, 165
Yorkshire Pudding, 139

SOUPS
Broccoli Cheese Soup, 116
Ham & Cheese Chowder, 123
Italian Sausage Soup, 128
Mom's Manhattan Clam Chowder, 125
Potato Soup, 120
Zesty Vegetable Soup, 121

...ts ☆ roast turkey ☆ sleigh rides ☆ caroling

wooly mittens ☆ silent nights ☆ snowball fights ☆ plum pudding ☆ ginger

bread men ☆ popcorn garlands ☆ cutting the tre...

hot cocoa ☆ company's coming ☆ snow angels ☆ handmade ornaments

...ts ☆ roast turkey ☆ sleigh rides ☆ caroling

wooly mittens ☆ silent nights ☆ snowball fights ☆ plum pudding ☆ ginger

bread men ☆ popcorn garlands ☆ cutting the tre...

☆ hot cocoa ☆ company's coming ☆ snow angels ☆ handmade ornaments

Gooseberry Patch Originals

WELCOME HOME for the HOLIDAYS

your companion from ★ September through December

Welcome Home For The Holidays

No from harvest through Christmas... a treasury of holiday recipes, decorating tips, traditions & easy-to-make gifts

Old-Fashioned Country Christmas

A holiday keepsake of recipes, traditions, homemade gifts, decorating ideas, & favorite childhood memories

OLD-FASHIONED COUNTRY COOKIES

hundreds of recipes, tips, & ideas

Old-Fashioned Country Cookies

Yummy recipes, tips, traditions, how-to's, and sweet memories... everything Cookies

OLD-FASHIONED COUNTRY CHRISTMA

our all-time BEST SELLER

GOOD FOR YOU!

recipes, fun ideas, heartwarming stori good for body, mind, s

FOR BEES & ME 🐝

garden-fresh recipes, backyard entertaining & gifts from the garden

For Bees & Me

A Bouquet of Garden-Fresh Recipes, Menus, Hints, Simple Pleasures, Herbal Beauty Potions, Backyard Entertainment & Easy-To-Make Gifts

Good For You!

A collection of good food, good fun, & good stories for the body, mind & soul!

☆ handmade ornaments ☆ roast turkey ☆ sleigh rides ☆ caroling ☆ wooly mittens ☆ silent nights ☆ snowball fights ☆ plum pudding ☆ gingerbread men ☆ popcorn garlands ☆ cutting the tree ☆ hot cocoa ☆ company's coming ☆ snow angels ☆

Gooseberry Patch
149 Johnson Drive
Department BOOK
Delaware, OH 43015

...try Store In Your Mailbox®

ease send me the following Gooseberry Patch books:

ook	Quantity	Price	Total
d-Fashioned Country Christmas	_____	$14.95	_____
elcome Home for the Holidays	_____	$14.95	_____
d-Fashioned Country Cookies	_____	$14.95	_____
r Bees & Me	_____	$17.95	_____
od For You!	_____	$14.95	_____
mespun Christmas	_____	$14.95	_____
lebrate Spring	_____	$12.95	_____
lebrate Summer	_____	$12.95	_____
lebrate Autumn	_____	$12.95	_____
lebrate Winter	_____	$12.95	_____
ming Home for Christmas	_____	$14.95	_____
mily Favorites	_____	$14.95	_____
ckyard Gatherings	_____	$14.95	_____
lidays at Home	_____	$14.95	_____
untry Friends™ Good Times	_____	$14.95	_____

Merchandise Total _____

Ohio Residents add 6 1/4% _____

Shipping & handling: Add $2.50 for each book. Call for special delivery prices. _____

Total _____

*Quantity discounts and special shipping prices available when purchasing
6 or more books. Call and ask! Wholesale inquiries invited.*

Name: _____

Address: _____

City: _____ State: _____ Zip: _____

ts ☆ roast turkey ☆ sleigh rides ☆ caroling

☆ hot cocoa ☆ company's coming ☆ snow angels ☆ handmade ornaments

...read men ☆ popcorn garlands ☆ cutting the tre...